BODY as SPIRIT

BODY as SPIRIT

The Nature
of Religious Feeling

by Charles Davis

A Crossroad Book
THE SEABURY PRESS · NEW YORK

The Seabury Press
815 Second Avenue
New York, N.Y. 10017

Printed in the United States of America

Library of Congress Cataloging in Publication Data

Davis, Charles, 1923-   Body as spirit.
   "A Crossroad book."
1. Christianity—Psychology. 2. Perception.
3. Experience (Religion) 4. Man (Theology)
I. Title.
BR110.D29   201   75-42023   ISBN 0-8164-0288-4

FOR FLORENCE,

WHO UNDERSTOOD
THE MEANING OF FEELING
BEFORE I DID.

Contents

I.
Feeling as the Human Response to Reality

A person who lacks feeling is out of touch with reality. Everyone recognizes the truth of that, at least for some circumstances. For example, in the family situation: a faithful husband and hard-working provider is still a foreigner in the home if he is insensitive to the unspoken or half-expressed attitudes, reactions, desires, and needs of his wife and children. He has to feel—he cannot simply be told—what is going on in and among the family members. If he does not, he is less than human—a stone lodged within the organism of the family. Again, in the wider social situation, most people have had experience of someone who in a committee or social gathering has no "feel" for the actualities of the situation and as a result behaves with clumsy ineptitude. Though perhaps brilliant intellectually, a person without feeling is blind and deaf to human reality.

What, then, is feeling? To get near so elusive a concept requires some distinctions. Feeling differs from the operational skills men develop. To watch a child growing up is to realize the many skills involved in ordinary human living, together with their complexity. Parents observe the gradual acquisition of muscular control in holding and manipulating objects and in walking, running, jumping, and climbing. Then comes the eye and hand coordination demanded by drawing and writing, followed by the perceptual and intellectual skills required for counting and reading. From basic skills men form ever more complex skills, grouping muscular, perceptual, imaginative, and intellectual operations. Skills are combined in sports and games, in arts and crafts, in industry and business, in sciences, in practical affairs. To watch great skill being exercised in a trained athlete or accomplished musician, for example, is to wonder at human achievement. But a highly skilled man may be and sometimes is deficient in feeling.

Feeling is not the same as intellectual activity. The word "intellectual" is narrower in meaning than "intelligent." Thus we use "intelligent feeling" to mean an affective response illumined by an understanding grasp of the situation; but "intellectual" generally implies a detachment that registers the facts or state of affairs while holding back from affective response and resultant action. To speak of intellectual activity is to refer to what engages only part of ourselves, and for that reason connotes only a limited awareness of reality. The frequent absorption of the intellectual in his problem is deceptive here. To be oblivious to all else in working out a mathematical or scientific problem does not mean that the total self is engaged, but merely that a functional narrowing of consciousness keeps much of the self dormant. The absorbed intellectual is not operating at the affective level, not, at least, apart from the intellectual drive itself as a passion for truth.

The restriction that a merely intellectual response implies is best seen in the social sciences. There the subject matter itself frequently calls for affective responses—such as indignation at injustice, desire for reform, enthusiasm for a movement, scorn for hypocrisy—and impels subsequent engagement in action. The social scientist, however, usually studies the issues without regarding such responses and action as belonging to his intellectual work as a scientist, even if he recognizes them as incumbent upon him as a citizen and a man. Nevertheless, it is only by such responses that the values inherent in a situation are revealed. A person who does not feel admiration for a good action or indignation at a bad action, who is utterly unmoved by instances of injustice or examples of selfless generosity, is simply not apprehending values. He is blind to them. But on that account he does not see reality aright. Values are not identical with our subjective responses but are features in reality to which we respond. What makes some of us confuse them with our responses is that the qualitative features of reality we call values only manifest themselves to us through our affective responses. Not to feel injustice is not to perceive injustice, even if we learn to name it from what others say. For that reason the intellectual approach to reality, being an incomplete response, reveals reality only partially.

To stop short of values in a merely intellectual attitude to reality may be legitimate in theoretical work as part of a useful distinguishing of successive tasks and concerns, provided the intellectual response is never taken as total. But if practical affairs are based upon intellectual activity alone, without feeling and therefore without regard to values, the individual becomes at worst a psychopath, at best a "wheeler-dealer," and society a monstrous mechanism.

Feeling should not be confused with emotion. Although "emotion" and "feeling" are often treated as synonyms, "emotion" directly refers to bodily agitation. A person is said to be under great emotion when much perturbed in body: sobbing or crying, shouting or screaming, breathing irregularly, or behaving in some similar fashion. And even when emotions are not violent, as a rule they are identified with changes in the bodily organism.

Feelings do include the emotions as their bodily component, but "feeling" directly refers, not to the organic reverberations of our affective life, but to our affective responses when understood as conscious, insightful responses to intelligently grasped situations. When we speak of feeling, we imply an element of rational appreciation of what is felt. Hence, strength of feeling and vehemence of emotion do not always correspond. Commercial entertainment plays upon the emotions— exciting the sensations associated with love, tenderness, sorrow, dread, horror, and so forth—without genuine feelings, because intelligent appreciation of the situation is deliberately smothered rather than evoked. To arouse strong feelings by an art that is true to the reality of human existence is considered, not without reason, as too disturbing for individuals—"human kind cannot bear very much reality,"[1] T. S. Eliot said—and too threatening to the established social and political order. Consequently, people are offered every emotional excitement and thrill, while their feelings are kept dormant or deadened. Commercialized sex is a good example of emotion without feeling.

Where feelings differ from emotions, then, is in their being spiritual and rational in their animating core. The word "rational" will cause a negative reaction in some people, who will take it as a virtual denial of the distinctive place and function of feeling as feeling. However, it is a mistake to oppose affectivity and rationality. The heart may have its reasons which reason does not know, as Pascal says; but it does have reasons. Genuine affective responses are rational.

Thus, Erich Fromm in *The Art of Loving* argues that love must be objective or else it is no more than narcissistic self-deception. Pointing out that reason is the faculty to think objectively, he states: "To have acquired the capacity for objectivity and reason is half the road to achieving the art of loving."[2] He is reiterating what we all know: to love without the objectivity that opens us to truth is to love our own fantasies, not the reality of the other person.

Similarly, Arthur Janov in *The Primal Scream* defines feeling as "sensation conceptualized" and adds: "This means correctly conceptualized."[3] The method he developed as primal therapy rests upon the conviction that neurosis is due to a refusal of feeling. Some pain is too intolerable to be borne in childhood, and so the child avoids it by refusing to feel. If the refusal cuts deep enough, the child goes so far as to shut off the reality of its own needs and desires, defending itself by hiding behind an unreal or neurotic self. Thus, locked up in each neurotic is a pool of primal pain—the pain the neurotic refused to feel in the past. For the cure of the neurosis, that pain must be released by being actually felt. It must be felt, not just known; but it is felt only if the sensation is correctly conceptualized. The pain must not be disguised under some false, anaesthetizing conceptualization, but felt as what it truly is in reality. For example, the child may have refused to feel the painful lack of a warm, affectionate father because to feel it for what it was would have been unbearable to the point of destruction. But now for the adult to cure the resultant neurosis, that pain must be unlocked and felt fully. Primal therapy is designed to provoke the release of the pain. This usually occurs in a shattering experience, namely the primal scream—literally a scream.

For Janov, then, feeling is a total experience in which body and mind are joined. That is why for him body techniques such as dance therapy on the one hand, and mental techniques such as psychoanalysis on the other, are insufficient. There must be a total response that again unifies the person. Feelings, we may conclude so far, are responses that are total. A feeling differs from mere emotion in being an intelligent, insightful relationship with what is felt. It is not just a bodily reaction to a physical or imaginative stimulus. It is a spiritual, rational response, implying a cognitive apprehension of the object. At the same time, it is an affective response; it differs from the detached observation, assessment, and judgment we call intellectual. Again, the appetency or affectivity from which feelings arise, while intelligent and spiritual, is also at once bodily. There is no feeling without bodily motion, any more than there is intellectual knowledge without the participation of sense and imagination. In the unity of a single response, feeling is both intelligent and visceral.

Feelings may best be described as responses springing from what we are. They are responses of our being to reality as we meet it. Our feeling responses, their range and quality, depend upon what we have become as beings, what we are as persons. Our responses will indeed be mistaken if there is a misapprehension of the facts, but feeling remains genuine if the response comes from what we are. For example, someone told wrongly that his friend has died will genuinely though mistakenly mourn. On the other hand, feelings cease to be genuine if the actual response of our being to some object or event is suppressed or hidden from consciousness and replaced by the words, gestures, and motions of a stock response borrowed from others or an invented, fake response of our own. People do become cut off from their real feelings. They even cease to feel truly. Their real selves are then concealed by a cloud of counterfeit feelings; that is, responses not arising from their own encounter with reality but simulated to conform to what they think others expect of them, or responses unconsciously devised to serve as camouflages hiding feelings of which they are afraid from themselves and others.

At this point we must look more closely at the function of conceptualization and language in relation to feelings. I am not entirely happy with Janov's definition of feeling as sensation correctly conceptualized. The definition identifies the intelligent element in feeling with concepts. Prior to any conceptual formulation, however, there is the direct, intelligent apprehension of the object, the insightful grasp of what is felt. Intelligence is present and operative even before the mind formulates in concepts what is intelligently apprehended, and the intelligent grasp of the object may and often does run deeper than what can be clearly formulated. Feelings are spontaneous responses; they are the stirring of our intelligent, spiritual, embodied affectivity toward whatever is presented to it. I have argued that affective responses are themselves cognitive insofar as they reveal those features of reality we call values. Nevertheless, feelings presuppose as already given a factual presentation of the object. Hence, to the extent that the factual presentation requires and includes concepts, judgments, words, and other expressions, feelings will follow upon those. Our aesthetic feelings in relation to a play or novel, and our moral feelings in relation to a social situation, presuppose an elaborate presentation in concepts and words. But the feelings themselves, if really the movement of our affectivity, are sound and genuine even before any conceptualization of the values felt or any objectification in concepts of the feelings as responses.

All the same, feelings are inchoate until developed, crude until educated; and conceptualization and language are necessary for their development and education. We grow in knowledge only by learning to formulate each step in concepts and words. If our knowledge is to advance, the flow of expression must continue and increase. A block in expression checks the process of knowing. The same is true on the level of affectivity. Feelings do not blossom until a range of expression, both in concepts and words, allows us to discriminate among values and to distinguish different responses by naming them. Feelings are indeed spontaneous, but we still have to learn to feel, because our spontaneity is not a fixed quantity. It grows as we grow. We have to educate and differentiate our feelings by being alert to their movements, noticing and approving some while ignoring and disapproving others. That, incidentally, is the way we educate children, as well as ourselves, in their feeling responses. But to give formative attention to feelings implies being able to name them correctly or, what comes to the same thing, being able to conceptualize every shade of feeling precisely. In brief, if intelligence and affectivity have an originative, responsive power prior to conceptualization and language, they remain stunted and rudimentary until joined in an indissoluble union with the flow of the concepts and words that express and preserve each phase of their movement.

Without expression, then, both intelligence and affectivity would remain largely potential. At the same time, the necessity for conceptualization and language introduces a great danger, because we borrow our concepts and words from those around us. It is from other people that we learn concepts, conceptual systems, words, metaphors, language structures, and literary forms. They are the product of other people's experience and mental activity. To serve as genuine expressions for ourselves, they should be linked with our own experience and mental activity and become products in turn of our own intelligence and affectivity. Instead, they frequently remain intrusions from without, extraneous to our own creative responses, and their effect is not to release and foster but to smother our own intelligent and affective spontaneity. Some children have imposed upon them a ready-made structure of thoughts and feelings when they are growing up, and they never learn to recognize the workings of their own minds or to trust their own feelings. Every university teacher has met the student who can skillfully manipulate complex conceptual systems but has no intelligent grasp of the questions the systems were devised to deal with. Premature and unskillful instruction in literary criticism often blocks a person's own aesthetic responses to great literature. Thus, concepts and words so easily become tools for manufacturing sham thoughts and counterfeit feelings.

Thus Janov is right to insist upon correct conceptualization in the process of therapy. Whenever genuine feelings have been suppressed and covered over by fake, substitute feelings, it is necessary to engage in a process of reappropriating the buried feelings. This can be done only by objectifying them in a correct conceptualization so that they are recognized and accepted for what they were and are. They have been concealed by a false conceptualization; they must be brought into the open by being correctly conceptualized. In other words, the therapeutic process like education takes place in and through expression in concepts and words—with, of course, in primal therapy, the appropriate bodily component. However, I still want to insist that feelings are intelligent responses, not just bodily sensations, in the first spontaneous movement preceding conceptualization.

Feelings, I have said, are responses springing from what we are. They are the eros of our being when that being is aroused by its interaction with reality. Feelings are the actuation of our nature, our capacities, our dispositions, our habits; they are the awakening of ourselves as subjects by the objects that come before us and act upon us. We use the word "feeling" of the responses that are total insofar as they come from the unity of the self as an embodied person or personal body. Feelings are bodily responses that are animated by intelligence and spiritual affectivity or, conversely, embodied intelligent and affective responses.

The word "feeling" is commonly used, first, of responses motivated by the pleasurable or subjectively satisfying; second, of aesthetic responses to the beautiful; and third, of responses motivated by values, namely by what is good in itself independently of the subject. It is unusual to speak of feeling in regard to the response to truth. Yet there is reason to do so, and to consider why will further illuminate the function of feeling.

Behind the cognitive process is an eros for the truth, a desire to know. The subject seeking knowledge must have an active orientation toward truth; he must have that within him which personally and creatively responds to its presence. Without a positive capacity that, as it were, vibrates in harmony with the truth being sought, a person would not recognize the true when he met it.

To put this more concretely: How, for instance, does a person understand a given object or set of data? Not by passively receiving impressions, but by actively leaping to grasp the meaning in the presentation. The mind, we can say, gives a bound and grasps the sense of what comes before it. The teacher has to wait patiently for that personal response, doing his best to facilitate it by varying the presentation. But until the mind's intrinsic feel for meaning is actuated, there is no understanding. Meaning must be felt; it cannot be just registered. Again, before making a judgment, a person must grasp the sufficiency of the evidence; mechanical checking will not do. Grasping evidence as sufficient demands a response or movement of the subject in which previous experience, knowledge, and habits all play their part. A trained scientist has a feel for what counts as scientific evidence and an historian for what is enough to establish an historical fact. Granted they must be able to display the warrants on which they rest their judgments to their colleagues; yet they themselves are able fully to appreciate the strength of those warrants only by what they have become as scientists and historians.

To put it in another way, it is possible to check the

formal, logical correctness of an argument without any
personal involvement that could be called feeling. A
machine could do it perfectly. But the cognitive process,
when considered as a search for truth, as a grasp of
meaning, or as a recognition of the sufficiency of evidence for affirming a fact, is essentially a matter of personal response, dependent upon what the subject is and
has become. For that reason we can rightly speak of an
eros for truth and see our apprehension of truth as a
function of feeling.

Nor is the body excluded from the cognitive process
but is intimately involved at every stage. To make the
point briefly in a sentence of W. B. Yeats: "We only
believe those thoughts which have been conceived not in
the brain but in the whole body."[4]

Intellectual activity has commonly been set apart
from feelings, because up to a point—and it is only up to a
point—the desire and feeling for truth can be operative
in isolation; that is, without affecting the values by which
we live, without making personal demands upon our
responsibility and freedom, and, consequently, while
leaving untouched the higher levels of our spiritual affectivity. In contrast, the feelings through which we
apprehend moral values do create serious demands
upon us for responsible decision and action. When we
fail to act according to the moral values we apprehend,
we diminish those same values in their presence within us
as qualities of our being and originative of our feelings.
There must be some justice within a man for him to
recognize what is just. To act unjustly is to become less
just and that much less capable of apprehending justice
again. Moral feelings are weakened or strengthened by
subsequent action. The pursuit of truth likewise requires
a harmony between subject and object, which can be
strengthened or weakened. But moral values are more
subjective, not in the sense of lacking objectivity, but
because they involve more of the subject for that con-

natural response which reveals their objective presence. Moral feelings as a consequence are more vulnerable, more exposed to distortion and corruption, more liable to suppression than the feelings operative in the kind of intellectual activity that leaves our lives unaffected and unchallenged.

Aesthetic feelings in this respect come between intellectual and moral feelings. They involve more of the subject than intellectual responses and are consequently considered more subjective. However, the struggle of artists for a compelling rightness in their work, the way beauty takes us out of ourselves and the agreed recognition of masterpieces, all give the lie to the contention that beauty is a mere matter of personal taste. It has its own objectivity. The element of truth in this contention is that the feeling for beauty when it is the discriminating response of a fine sensibility requires a considerable prior formation of the subject. All the same, aesthetic values as such stand at some distance from action and living; aesthetic feelings do not directly engage our responsibility and freedom. Admittedly, our relation to art is rarely a purely aesthetic one. Discussions of the modern novel, for example, show that moral and religious values also are at issue. Moreover, artistic works always have subtle, indirect effects on convictions and conduct. Nevertheless, aesthetic responses of themselves do not require the same degree of personal commitment as moral feelings for their functioning and development.

But it is time to return to the main point. I am trying to elucidate the concept of feeling. In doing so, I am arguing against the dichotomy usually made between intelligence and feeling, between rationality and feeling. As soon as the importance of feeling is stressed, some fear a denigration of reason and an invitation to every irrational excess. Conversely, an emphasis upon reason is seen by others as a suppression of affective and moral involvement in favor of a cold-blooded, amoral, computerlike manipulation of facts and figures. Both reactions are extreme and have in common a refusal to acknowledge the unity of the human response to reality, a unity found in feeling as a response both intelligent and affective, both rational and emotional.

There are grounds—and I have stated them—for distinguishing between feelings and intellectual activity. Briefly, again, "feelings" refers to a total response, actuating what we are as persons; intellectual activity is a restricted response, engaging neither the total self nor the total reality of the object. But there is no complete or basic distinction between the intellectual and the affective, because an affectivity toward truth underlies and penetrates the intellect as creative or originative in each person. The appropriate distinction needed to locate feeling precisely is not between intelligence and affectivity but between the spontaneous, connatural response of the subject to reality as object and the subsequent appropriation and formulation of that response in conceptualization and judgment. The first, connatural response, is what is rightly called feeling, whether the response is to reality as truth, as beauty, or as goodness.

Feelings, therefore, may be defined in terms of a connaturality that exists between human subjects and objective reality. Knowledge, whether of facts or of values, is the achievement of an enriching connection between human subjects as poor, incomplete, potential beings and the reality they need to complete, actuate, and make them whole. A feeling is the actuation in a spontaneous movement of response of the mutual, connatural relation between human beings as subjects and the reality they meet as objects. It is the expression of the oneness between the heart of man (the spirit within) and the heart of reality (the truth, beauty, and goodness which is the spirit in the world). Since the human self is both intelligent and bodily, spiritual and material, its spontaneous responses are indissolubly both intelligent and bodily, spiritual and physiological.

The moment of spontaneity in the human response

to reality is at once followed by a movement to fix and formulate the response in concepts and judgments. In seeking factual knowledge, we respond connaturally to meaning in the data and then formulate that meaning in concepts and words. Again, we respond to the sufficiency of evidence and then formulate our response in judgments of facts. On a higher level of consciousness, values are revealed and apprehended in spontaneous responses originating in the subject as possessing corresponding values. It is these responses to values that are called feelings in the strict sense. Feelings, thus, are the arousal of our spiritual affectivity by objective reality as having those qualities, namely values, to which affective responses are appropriate. The subject formulates feelings in a variety of expressions. But a further step is needed. Feelings as a spontaneous awareness of values have to be examined in relation to their objective reference; in brief, there must be a movement of reflexive discrimination, corresponding to the weighing of sufficiency of evidence at the factual level and leading to an acknowledgement of the objective presence of particular values, which is then formulated in a judgment of value.

Since any single instance of response to meaning or value is but a moment in an ongoing process of knowledge or affective life, the spontaneous movements become inextricably intertwined with the elements of formulation and expression. Each spontaneous response depends upon the formulation of a previous response and leads to a subsequent formulation, and so on. I have already noted how the development of knowledge and the education of feeling depend upon conceptualization and expression. There is no question, therefore, of marking off a realm of intuitive knowledge and spontaneous feelings from a separate realm of conceptual thought and judgments of fact or value. The connatural responses of intelligence and affectivity to reality, and the effort to fix and formulate those responses in concepts and judgments, are both parts of the conscious, meaningful relation of the human subject to reality. Without spontaneous, personal responses, intelligence ceases to be creative and becomes degraded into a calculative skill used to manipulate concepts and propositions, and the affective life loses authenticity and becomes a stage for the display of borrowed and counterfeit feelings. Contrariwise, without the work of formulation, intelligence remains a bright promise clouded in vagueness, a potentiality without achievement, an affectivity crude and undiscriminating, a sensibility without maturity.

Feelings, the resonance of reality upon human subjects, are distinguished in their originality by spontaneity and immediacy. A word about each of the two is needed. We cannot directly summon up feelings. Only indirectly do they come under our deliberate choice. Feelings that are genuine and not pretended arise from what we are, from what we have become, and do so without deliberation or choice. In that sense they are spontaneous. But that does not mean that they entirely escape our responsibility and freedom. We are responsible for what we have become; to a considerable degree we freely make ourselves. The way we have acted in the past largely determines how we feel in the present. And feelings can be educated and purified. Attention and approval will reinforce some; neglect and disapproval will weaken others. Careful study of the objects to which they refer can also make them more discriminating; thus, the study of art may refine aesthetic sensibility. In brief, at any particular time, spontaneity is a given for the present, but a task for the future.

The variability of spontaneity as the source of feelings and the possibility of immaturity and corruption point to the need for discernment in judging feelings and following them with action. The mere fact of positive feelings is not a guarantee of reaching truth, goodness, or beauty. Questions that are relevant here are: Who is it that feels? What is the purity and growth of the feeling subject? These questions have to be asked about ourselves as well as about others. In other words, there is room for what religious writers, in dealing with spiritual affections, call "the discernment of spirits."

That does not mean that we can turn away from the subjective self, with its imperfections and corruptions, and find security from mistakes in an appeal to external norms. External norms provide useful guidance; feelings do demand a sustained social context for their growth and purification. But external norms themselves become misunderstood and corrupted unless there are genuine human subjects to receive and interpret them. The basic solution is to be found in the unity of subjectivity and objectivity. Human feelings, by their dynamism, point beyond themselves; they are an expression of self-transcendence; they take us, as we say, out of ourselves; that is, into truth, goodness, and beauty. The discernment of spirits, the education and purification of feelings are fundamentally matters of uncovering and releasing that dynamic self-transcendence, of allowing it its full range, so that it overcomes the self-centeredness, the unobjectivity of a retreat out of reality into an unreal, egotistic world characteristic of immaturity and corruption. Oneness with objective reality is not achieved by an external, supposedly invariable, impersonal standard, but by the purified wholeness and unnarrowed receptivity of a responsive subject.

The second characteristic of feelings is their immediacy. The meaning is clear enough: feelings directly relate the subject to reality. To feel is to respond to the reality of the object, not to concepts or words about it. The contrast here is between a responsive union with some concrete, present reality and a concern with an object at one or several removes in an indirect relationship. The point may be illustrated with reference to a work of art. A feeling response is a relation with the work of art itself. But it is possible to talk about it, to read art critics on it, to know indeed a great deal about it without any direct responsive relationship with the concrete reality of the work itself. Again, to be religious, as I shall argue, is to have religious feelings, but it is possible to be a student of religion, to know much about religion without having the religious feelings that relate the person directly to the reality with which religion is concerned.

But the word "immediate" is misleading; indeed, inaccurate. Understood strictly, it would exclude any mediation. But feelings are not unmediated. At every stage of development beyond the confined consciousness of the infant, feelings are mediated by a complex context, both social and individual. A developed sensibility depends upon a flow of gestures, images, symbols, concepts, words, convictions, judgments, decisions, actions, and institutions. The music-lover listening to Bach, or the Christian believer participating in a Eucharist, responds by feelings which depend upon a mediation formed over centuries of cultural history. The question, however, remains valid: Are they responding to the concrete reality of the object presented, and thus entering into a direct, personal relationship with it? Or, are the mediating elements themselves the object of attention, so that the relationship with the mediated reality has become indirect? There is, in other words, a mediated immediacy, in which the mediating elements are transparent, facilitating and not blocking a direct relationship with the object. Despite the necessity of mediation, feelings, then, may be called immediate as being direct responses to objects in their concrete reality, not an indirect, abstract relationship, with representative elements taking the place of the real objects.

"Modern theologians," writes Herbert Richardson, "tend toward consensus that an irreducible element in 'true religion' is a certain feeling."[5] A conviction of the centrality of feeling in religion as well as in human living as a whole has provoked the present study. So, after the general consideration of feeling, questions must now be raised about religious feeling or feelings. But is there a distinctive feeling or range of feelings we can mark off as religious?

Several problems surround the use of the word "religion." The first is that of "the religions." Wilfred Cantwell Smith in *The Meaning and End of Religion*[6] has severely criticized the usage by which we speak of "religions" and give them names, such as Christianity, Buddhism, and so on. Briefly, the objections are:

(1) It causes a reification, which means a false assumption that there are real entities, such as Christianity and Buddhism, with unchanging essences about which we can make precise statements. There are no such entities. For Cantwell Smith, what corresponds in the real order to the confused mental construct of a "religion,"—Christianity, for example—is the varying personal faith of many individuals and the cumulative tradition resulting from that faith. But the replacement of "religion" by "personal faith" and "cumulative tradition" does not take account of the elements of community, institutions, and organization that come between personal faith and a cumulative tradition. Further, "the faith of Christians" and "the Christian tradition" would each seem to be open to the same danger of reification; namely, of being taken as a concrete entity with a single essence, as "the Christian religion."

(2) The boundaries between the different religions are blurred, especially when considered historically. They are also likely to become increasingly fluid as inter-religious contacts and influences multiply.

(3) Each religion is a complex set of elements—mystical, mythical, doctrinal, ritualistic, magical, political, psychotherapeutic, scientific, philosophical, and so

on. Both the selection and differentiation of elements vary from one so-called religion to another. It is impossible, therefore, to compare religions as if they were manifestations of an identical set of needs or activities.

(4) There are other ways of dividing religious phenomena, more profound and useful than the haphazard application of history and geography which has produced the grouping into the so-called religions of the world. For example, Max Weber's typology of religions as schemes of salvation cuts across the boundaries of "the religions."[7] Likewise, the distinction between mystical and prophetic religion produces a different grouping than the usual one of world religions.[8]

Those last three objections show how blunt an instrument of analysis the conventional division of religions is, and they warn against any great reliance upon it. However, in spite of the objections, it is unlikely that people in the near future will cease to speak of the "religions of the world," listing them according to the present grouping. The usage has sufficient truth, more in the case of some religions than others, to serve as a first descriptive grouping of phenomena.

The second problem about the use of the word "religion" is more relevant to our present purpose. Is there an element common and essential to all religions that justifies calling each of them "a religion"?

It is not necessary to suppose so. The use of the word "religion" does not demand the presence of some common, central element. Ninian Smart appeals here to Wittgenstein's notion of family resemblance.[9] Wittgenstein refers to the use of the word "game." When we look at the various proceedings we call "games," we do not find anything common to all, but "a complicated network of similarities overlapping and criss-crossing." In other words, no single feature is found in all games, but some games have a feature in common and they are severally related to other games by a different common feature. A complex pattern of overlapping features or set of "family resemblances" results. Thus there is no common essence of game, but games form a family. We can speak in the same way of "religions," not by virtue of a common essential element, but because of a "family resemblance." Some, indeed, remain content with a family resemblance among religions, and say there is no common phenomenon we can identify and discuss as religious experience, religious faith, or religious feeling.

William James in his classic study, *The Varieties of Religious Experience,* maintained that "the word 'religion' cannot stand for any single principle or essence, but is rather a collective name."[10] Pointing to the different ways of conceiving "religious sentiment," he argued against the idea that it was one specific thing. "Religious sentiment" is "a collective name for the many sentiments which religious objects may arouse in alternation." It "probably contains nothing whatever of a psychologically specific nature." Religious fear, religious love, religious awe, religious joy, and so forth, are man's ordinary, natural emotions directed to a religious object. Further, just as there is no one religious emotion, so also there would seem to be "no one specific and essential kind of religious object and no one specific and essential kind of religious act."[11]

There are two different contentions in this passage from William James. The first is that the word "religion" covers such a variety of phenomena that no one element can be singled out as common and essential. The second is that what are designated as religious feelings are psychologically the same as ordinary feelings and are distinctively religious only because of their object. Only the first contention concerns us here; the second will be taken up later.

Ninian Smart in the essay, "Truth and Religion," lays down the principle that the "phenomenological judgement as to whether there is a basic common core of religious experience must be based on the facts, and not determined *a priori* by theology." He then goes on to state his own view that "there is no such common core, but rather that there are different sorts of religious experience which recur in different traditions, though not universally."[12] In reply it could be said that while any phenomenological judgment must be based upon the facts, there would seem to be no good reason to exclude philosophy and theology from establishing an antecedent probability in this matter. I do not myself know of any phenomenological investigation or judgment so indisputably clear that it should predetermine the direction of philosophical and theological reflection. Such reflection, in my opinion, leads one to suppose universal features in religious experience.

Philosophically, one can argue that the fundamental structures of human existence are universal and, consequently, that a common basic pattern underlies the concrete diversity of human experience. That is what we commonly suppose. Thus, when we take for granted the possibility of communication among all men, we are implying a universal structure of human intelligence. Again, the many efforts to establish a unity among peoples by eliciting and fostering a measure of moral consensus presuppose a basic community of moral life among all men. The same general understanding of a fundamental unity among men of different cultures leads us to expect a common basic pattern in human religious experience.

Theologically, from a Christian standpoint it is difficult not to allow that God makes himself in some way or other accessible to all men. Christian belief as traditionally interpreted is in fact incompatible with the contention that groups of men have in their experience nothing that can be interpreted as a relationship with God.

While such philosophical and theological considerations should lead us to look more carefully at the facts, they should not be allowed to distort those facts. Better to remain with an unsolved problem than to pretend that the facts are other than what they are. Thus the immense difference between the Christian worship of a personal God and the aspiration toward nirvāna in Theravāda Buddhism demands recognition. The two are conceptually and in practice very far apart.

That difference is indeed the chief reason why Ninian Smart rejects the unity of religious experience. In *The Yogi and the Devotee* he is prepared to argue for a single basic mystical experience, so that the various types of mysticism—for example, the theistic and the monistic—are then taken as differing solely in interpretation, not in experience.[13] But in that book and in his other writings he strongly insists upon a phenomenological difference between two kinds of religious experience, the devotional and the mystical. The devotional type of religion, characteristic of Indian bhakti groups and of the Semitic religions, makes worship central, and even in the highest flights of loving union retains a sense of the distance between man and God. It is an experience of the numinous, in which God is always the Other. The mystical type of religion makes contemplative experience *(dhyāna)* central and moves toward an identification with the transcendent.

The existence of this mystical type in a pure form in Theravāda Buddhism leads Ninian Smart to deny any common core of religious experience. Even so, he is willing to admit that "though the central content of the Buddhist mystic's experience on the one hand and that of Muhammad's prophetic experience on the other hand differ greatly, there is in both the sense of a transcendent being or state, as though somehow here both had an insight into what lay, so to speak, beyond space and time." But this is evaluated as merely a "loose similarity."[14]

Why? Here it becomes clear that Ninian Smart's

account of devotional and mystical religious experience is not a mere statement of facts. It includes his estimation that the phenomenological difference between worship and contemplation—that is, between numinous experience and mystical identification—is more important than the phenomenological similarity of each having a transcendent focus. I disagree with that assessment. For me, the fact that both experiences relate to the transcendent, however differently conceived, is a more basic feature than any of their differences. It marks off both types of experience from other levels of human experience, whether intellectual, practical, aesthetic, or moral.

Admittedly, there is an ambiguity in the idea of a common core of religious experience. It can be taken as implying that one can isolate a concrete common element from different complex sets of religious activities. In that fashion every eucharistic liturgy includes as a common element the eating of sacred bread and the drinking of sacred wine, however different the ritual in which these actions are embedded. There is in that sense, it seems, no common core of religious experience across the different religions; indeed, one might be hard put to find such a common feature as central in the religious experience of all groups within a single major religious tradition. But the affirmation of a common core may be taken as the discernment of a common essence, the apprehension of a set of features as universal and essential, though found only in a variety of particular concrete realizations. That is what allows one to speak of a common human experience or a common moral experience. To restrict oneself in these cases to a family resemblance and to hold that the distinctively human or distinctively moral experiences of men are related only by a network of overlapping similarities with no universal features is to fall into nominalism. Nominalism, which restricts our knowledge to discrete particulars, does not adequately account for the actual workings of human intelligence, which proceeds by discerning common structures and meaning in the manifold of particulars.

I want, therefore, to maintain that there are universal features in religious experience, so that we can speak of a basic common pattern underlying the concrete diversity of the central experiences in the different religious traditions. Those universal features mark off religious experience from the other levels of human experience. In other words, religious experience constitutes a distinctive mode of human consciousness and living.

It is one thing in principle to hold a common basic structure in all religious experiences and another thing to discern that structure accurately and formulate it satisfactorily. Attempts so far to do so—for example, Rudolf Otto's classic study, *The Idea of the Holy*—have not succeeded in accounting adequately for all the concrete forms of religion. Nor do I expect to achieve an adequate analysis and formulation here. Apart from my being personally ill-equipped for such a task, phenomenological reflection upon religion is not yet sufficiently comparative to precisely delineate essential features common to the different religions. The following remarks on religious experience will therefore inevitably show their Western origin and context. Nevertheless, their purpose is to grasp basic features constitutive of religious experience as a distinctive realm of human existence. The hope is that the account will point, however approximately, to what in truth is structurally fundamental and consequently universal in the experience of religious man.

I think it useful at this point to make a distinction between religious experience and religious feeling. Religious experience, it seems to me, would be better used in a comprehensive sense of all the activities and passivities we call religious. It would therefore include the use of myth and symbol, participation in ritual, the following of mystical techniques, doctrinal beliefs; practical, social, and institutional activity, as well as the inner events of a religious consciousness. To confine religious experience, as is often done, to inner events is to create the false impression that the core of religion is a pure, unmediated, inward affair, all the rest being peripheral effect or expression. But this is to dehumanize religious experience. The inner events of religious living occur in and through bodily and symbolic, imaginative and conceptual activity; they are mediated. Taking part in the Eucharist, reading the Gospels, visiting the sick—all these and similar activities should be thought of as part of religious experience. Bearing insults without hatred, enduring sickness patiently, meeting failure with courage, facing death with hope—all these and similar passivities must be included in religious experience.

I would then use "religious feeling" to mean the element in religious experience of spontaneous, connatural response to religious reality, the vibration of our total being when we relate to the transcendent in and through religious activities and passivities. Religious feeling is the arousal of our personal being—our intelligent and bodily, spiritual and material selves—in what is, though variously mediated, a direct relation to transcendent reality. Religious feeling is constitutive of every truly personal religious experience, because without it religious responses are reduced to words, gestures, attitudes borrowed from others and repeated without personal involvement. By religious feeling a particular experience is intrinsically, not just extrinsically, for example merely verbally or socially religious.

The element of religious feeling may remain largely unnoticed as a quality of personal response hidden in a round of formal religious activities. This is often the case with people brought up religiously. They say their prayers, they attend services, they assent to a set of beliefs, they try to preserve religious and moral values in their daily lives, they may have emotional responses to religious music or the other externals of worship, but there is little personal sense of God. The presence of God is for them primarily a matter of belief, not of any direct sense of his mystery. The personal element of feeling is there, but as a low vibration or an almost unnoticed tug in the depths of the many religious activities, giving them a quality of personal meaningfulness they would otherwise lack.

With other people, or at a later stage in the lives of the religiously formal, religious feeling emerges— sometimes fleetingly, sometimes lastingly—as an explicit, recognizable element in religious living. There is then an express awareness of the transcendent. Such people are endowed with a personal religious sense. In other words, they have discerned and acknowledged a distinctive feeling, relating them directly to the reality with which their varied religious behavior is concerned. That religious feeling remains as the animating element in their many religious activities and passivities. When, however, it comes into view as a distinctive element, attention may be focused directly upon it. A person may suspend other activities in order to dwell with total concentration in a conscious relation to the transcendent.

The suspension of activities may extend to the suspension of all words, images, and concepts concerning transcendent reality itself. There is thus a withdrawal from the world of objects, not just from the objects of sense perception, but from all the intelligible objects making up the meaningful world of human knowing, willing, and doing. There is a withdrawal into a darkness of feeling beyond the world of formulated and formulable meaning.

The possibility of such a withdrawal confronts us with an essential and universal feature of religious feeling; namely, that its focus, or the term of its intentionality, is not a known object. (I am using the word "intentionality" here, not with reference to intention in the sense of purpose, but to refer to the directional nature of consciousness. Consciousness is always consciousness *of*—it has a direction and a term, that is, an intentionality.) The focus or term of conscious acts of feeling, knowing, willing, and doing in areas of human experience other than religious is a particular entity or value. Conscious acts "intend" objects. Consequently, there is a world of objects corresponding to the range of conscious acts. The transcendent, however, is not an object within the world of human meaning. Religious feeling, therefore, has an intentionality which plunges it into darkness and makes it a response to mystery.

It follows that religious images and concepts refer only indirectly to the transcendent. They are metaphors and analogies, not proper representations of transcendent reality. In other words, they do not arise from an intelligent grasp of what the transcendent is in itself, followed by the formulation of that insight in a mental representation. We cannot come to an understanding of the transcendent by laying hold of its reality as an object of thought. The function of religious images and concepts is to mediate the felt presence of a reality that remains unknown and to foster the appropriate affective response.

Feelings or affective responses are, I have already argued, themselves cognitive as revealing values. There is a knowledge that arises from love. In other words, values present within the subject and determining the quality of the subject's affectivity uncover corresponding values in the world of objects through the spontaneous, connatural responses the objects provoke. But ordinarily, feelings presuppose the factual presentation of objects and are responses to those objects. Religious feeling, on the contrary, runs ahead of factual knowledge and is the response to the pressure, as it were, of the unknown reality that lies beyond the world of objects. That reality is felt as a presence and a value, without being known as an object.

In brief, I am maintaining that a distinctive and universal characteristic of religious feeling is that it is a response to what lies beyond the whole world of apprehended objects. Despite the wealth and variety of images and concepts used to mediate it and indirectly to formulate its dynamic thrust and ultimate term, it remains essentially an affective response, a strange feeling of love and joy, in relation to an unknown transcendent.

Theists are those most likely to find such an account unsatisfactory. Is not God an object of knowledge? Do we not love him as a personal being? Has he not revealed himself?

The word "God" is properly used of the particular, theistic conception of transcendent reality, and only improperly is its meaning extended to include other conceptions of the Ultimate. In that sense, "God" does indeed designate an object of thought: namely, a supreme personal agent, the Creator, whom we worship; and an object of love, the supreme Thou, who calls us into a mutual personal relationship. All the same, the conception we name God, if it is not made an idol, must be recognized as merely an inadequate, analogical expression, mediating a thrust toward a directly inexpressible mystery that lies beyond any human conception. For that reason, the primary and fundamental reference of the word "God"—as of any other name for ultimate reality— is as pointing to the term or focus of the intentionality of religious consciousness toward mystery or the transcendent. In the last analysis, God, even for the theist, is not and cannot be an object in the world of human meaning. God as an object is an imaginative construct in stories intended to mediate a sense of the transcendent. And when the meaning implicit in those stories is analyzed in the form of doctrinal beliefs, the doctrines remain irreducibly metaphorical in their expression whenever they refer to God, his nature, attributes, and activity.

I would appeal here for support to the writings of the Christian mystics. This quotation from *The Cloud of*

Unknowing can stand for all the rest, because we are dealing with a commonplace of mystical writing:

> But now thou askest me and sayest: "How shall I think on himself, and what is he?" Unto this I cannot answer thee, except to say: "I know not."
>
> For thou has brought me with thy question into that same darkness, and into that same *cloud of unknowing*, that I would thou wert in thyself. For of all other creatures and their works—yea, and of the works of God himself—may a man through grace have fulness of knowing, and well can he think of them; but of God himself can no man think. And therefore I would leave all that thing that I can think, and choose to my love that thing that I cannot think. For why, he may well be loved, but not thought. By love may he be gotten and holden; but thought neither.[15]

In other words, God may be loved, but not, properly speaking, thought. He is reached by an affectivity that draws us beyond the whole world of human meaning, beyond all the objects of human thought. Unless the theist is willing to exclude the witness of the mystics as incompatible with his theism, he must relativize all his images and concepts of God, even those representing God as personal.

That does not mean that the theistic conception is a matter of indifference or that one conception of transcendent reality is as good as another. There is place for a discerning assessment of the images and concepts we use to formulate and regulate our sense of the transcendent and bring it into relation with other areas of our experience. The criteria for doing this are not, however, my present concern. The point I want to make here is that, even for the theist, religious feeling is fundamentally an affective response to an unknown reality lying beyond the entire world of human meaning and the objects of human thought. Further, the inability to make God properly an object of thought underlines for me the primacy of affectivity in religion.

That does not mean that any sense of the limits of human thought and meaning is already religious. To identify religious feeling more precisely, it is necessary to distinguish pre-religious feeling from religious feeling properly so called. I should classify as pre-religious all those feelings that express an awareness of human limits or finitude. They embody what may be called a negative sense of the nothingness surrounding human existence and human meaning. In whatever direction one follows the arrow of human striving and achievement, it plunges into a dark abyss, devoid of humanly apprehensible reality and meaning. Individual lives all come to an end, and with them cease all interpersonal relationships. Human societies come and go. Every human product eventually decays or is destroyed. The more knowledge grows, the more we are aware of its severe limits and relative value. Human life comes to be seen as an island of meaning set in a formless sea, a tiny patch illuminated by a flickering candle, around which men huddle to comfort themselves in the unmeaning dark.

I am marking out a general range of feeling, not attempting a detailed description of such feelings in the concrete. The sense of finitude has been expressed in various ways in literature and in philosophical and religious writing. The thin walls surrounding everyday existence collapse, and man is confronted by the limits that close in upon his existence and activity from every side.

That awareness of finitude is, in my opinion, pre-religious, and it does not always have a religious sequel. It may remain as a vague sense of depth, qualifying the superficiality of ordinary life and experience. It may result in a nihilistic option, in which man accepts final meaninglessness. In that option we confront ultimate absurdity, even while perhaps deciding to erect a fragile structure of meaning to dwell in before all human history is swallowed up by the meaningless flux of the universe.

Although not yet religious, the negative experience

of nothingness is preparatory to religious feeling, because it destroys the security of everyday life and thus opens the way to the transcendent. Religious feeling, however, does not stop at a sense of finitude. It emerges when the nothingness, the abyss empty of human meaning, is felt as utterly real and a source of bliss and joy. The nothingness is experienced as positive, as indeed more real than the objects of the world of human meaning. Religious feeling arises as a response. Despite the absence of humanly apprehensible reality or meaning, men find themselves drawn toward the nothingness as toward the supremely, though inexpressibly, real. The emptiness arouses deep positive affections, so that they embrace it as of surpassing value. The nothingness becomes mystery, a felt presence.

The affective awareness of mystery I have described in broad terms is found concretely in a range of feelings differing in emphasis and quality and mediated by many different images and conceptions. Some of its more general forms are a feeling of wholeness or totality, a feeling of depth, a sense of awe or of the holy, a feeling of absolute dependence, a feeling of ultimate rightness, a strange sense of objectless joy or bliss. Religious feeling may also be bound up with more specific conceptions of the transcendent, as when it becomes love of a personal God. There is room for great variety in the concrete manifestation of religious response to the all-encompassing yet unknown reality. What distinguishes all these feelings as essentially religious, however, is that they take man out of and beyond his ordinary self, out of and beyond the limited world in which he lives and open him to what is unlimited and unapprehensible, though felt as utterly real and blissful.

At this point we may return to the second question raised by the passage I quoted from William James: Are religious feelings psychologically the same as ordinary feelings and distinctively religious only because of their object? James, it will be remembered, considered it probable that religious sentiment contains nothing whatever that is psychologically specific, but consists of ordinary natural emotions directed to a religious object.

In reply I would first note how vague and crude is the naming and classification of feelings. We speak of desire, joy, esteem, love, admiration, fear, sorrow, contempt, hatred, dread, but each of these words embraces a great variety of feelings that are recognizably different to any moderately reflective consciousness. The joy of reconciliation with a friend after a quarrel is not the same as the joy experienced in writing when words and thoughts come happily together. The fear of punishment is not the same as the fear of hurting someone who is loved. We name and classify feelings according to wide generalizations. We distinguish feelings when the object is present, such as joy, from feelings when the object is absent, such as desire; and feelings expressing a positive evaluation, such as esteem and admiration, from feelings expressing a negative evaluation, such as contempt and hatred. The classes could hardly be broader. And the simple names for the feelings are so imprecise that to designate even differences everyone acknowledges we must describe the feeling, not just name it. The fact, then, that we use the same name for religious feelings as for others does not exclude a specific difference. Again, feelings are not purely subjective emotional states, but spiritual and intelligent responses. For that reason, even psychologically they are given their specific determination by their objects. They are intentional responses, using "intentional" as before to refer to the directional nature of conscious acts. It does not make sense, therefore, for James to distinguish religious feelings by their objects while saying that they have nothing of a psychologically specific nature. In the Scholastic adage: Actions are specified by their objects. Once admit that feelings are not just emotional states but conscious responses, and they become specified by their objects, even psychologically.

I have already indicated that religious feelings are distinguished by not having an object in the ordinary sense, but by being directed toward mystery as their term or focus. Their intentionality toward what transcends the world of objects gives them their specific nature. But the relation with transcendent reality is many-sided. The transcendent is both present and absent, and hence the source of both joy and desire; it is both hoped for and feared; it creates both a love of good and a hatred of evil; it makes us distrust our everyday self, but trust the deeper self within; and so on. In brief, the basic response or orientation to the transcendent refracts into a broad spectrum of feelings as it passes through the concrete reality and circumstances of human existence. Particular feelings become associated with particular images and concepts, rites and doctrines, institutions and traditions, among those mediating the relationship with the transcendent.

A single feeling as a total response, both bodily and spiritual, of the person is a complex reality composed of a number of elements. The elements are fused into a unity by the meaning animating the complex as a whole and making it a response of a specific kind. But some of the individual elements, considered in isolation from the whole, remain identically the same in different feelings. Thus, a bodily gesture, looked at simply as a bodily movement in isolation, is identically the same when part of an expression of friendship or of ironic contempt. However, when placed in its relation to the whole response, it becomes a specifically different gesture. Therefore, when James refers to a psychological identity between religious and other feelings, it is well to ask at what level he discriminates feelings and their constituents. A feeling as a complex total response may differ specifically from another feeling, while taking up into itself elements that, as elements, are psychologically the same in both.

Before concluding I want to note again that religious

feelings, in the sense I have defined them, may and often do remain largely unnoticed in the lives of many Christians. For these people religion is a round of ritual activities, moral imperatives, and doctrinal beliefs. They do frequently experience some emotion in their prayers and hymn-singing, but that is not what I mean by religious feeling. What they do not have, however, is an explicit, personal awareness of the presence of God. A conscious sense of transcendent mystery is not a distinctly recognizable element in their otherwise faithful and sincere religious practice. Nevertheless, unless that practice is purely external and formal, religious feelings are there. They are implicitly there as an operative though unrecognized quality, as precisely that element that makes the religious practice truly personal.

What my analysis means, then, is that mystical experience is not something apart from ordinary religion, but the coming into explicit consciousness of the primary constitutive element of all genuine religion; namely, religious feeling understood as an immediate, spontaneous, connatural response to transcendent reality. In the mystic, the awareness of mystery becomes explicit, and this allows it to dominate consciousness, sometimes absorbing it completely.

Thus, true religion is rooted primarily in the affections. It is the deepest arousal of our affectivity. How is it, then, that religion, mystical religion particularly, has—with reason—been seen as the enemy of the body and the affections?

II.
The Religious Refusal of the Body

An ancient and almost universal conviction sees a conflict between bodily, sensuous experience and the religious quest. To seek religious liberation means to renounce the body, its pleasures and affections, as far as possible, and to mortify—that is, deaden—the impulses that remain. Meister Eckhart puts it succinctly: "There is no physical or fleshly pleasure without some spiritual harm."[1] And John of the Cross would seem to exclude all bodily affectivity:

> The reason for which it is necessary for the soul, in order to attain to Divine union with God, to pass through his dark night of mortification of the desires and denial of pleasures in all things, is because all the affections which it has for creatures are pure darkness in the eyes of God, and when the soul is clothed in these affections, it has no capacity for being enlightened and possessed by the pure and simple light of God, if it first cast them not from it; for light cannot agree with darkness.[2]

He urges "the mortifying and calming of the four natural passions, which are joy, hope, fear and grief," so as to enter into "complete detachment and emptiness and poverty, with respect to everything that is in the world."[3]

I do not want to dwell here upon the cruder forms of religious hostility to the body. That much religion fears the body is now a hackneyed observation, especially since the general rejection of the traditional views on sex. There has, in fact, been so much talk about the anti-body attitude of religion that what began as a sound reaction has hardened into an undiscriminating prejudice. The problem, however, is deeper and more subtle than a moral shrinking from sexuality.

Mystics and others pursuing holiness or spiritual liberation would not, it seems, agree with my giving a central place to religious feelings, nor with my understanding of religious affections as total responses, bodily as well as spiritual, sensuous as well as intelligent. I have argued that the fundamental religious experience is the total, connatural response of ourselves as embodied persons to religious reality and value. It would follow that we should encourage and train the bodily component of our affectivity, direct and refine it, so that it becomes the medium of spiritual meaning. Instead, we are met, apparently, with a negation of bodiliness and sensuousness. We are asked to exclude our affectivity. There is little or no acknowledgement of the processes of material mediation implied by our complex makeup as embodied persons. In brief, there is seemingly a reaching after a pure immateriality of religious response.

Is this just a refusal of the body? Or, is this not rather a refusal of the spirit? I mean this: If the body is seen merely as a sensual obstacle to the spirit, it is being refused as a manifestation of the spirit. Consequently, the spirit in one of its forms is being rejected. To understand this, we must first turn to another form of the refusal of the body.

Among the many communes of our time, there was one where the members went around naked. It was reported that their nudism was found offensive by their neighbors. This was not, of course, surprising, but what drew my attention to the news item was a remark made by one of the complainants. The people in the commune were of different ages and of various shapes and sizes. They were not a group of pin-up beauties. The complainant remarked that he would not have minded had they been beautiful to look at, like the playmates of *Playboy*, but that he found the naked bodies of these people ugly and repulsive.

The willingness to gaze pleasurably upon the nudes in *Playboy* or *Penthouse* and to enjoy the sight of shapely girls in bikinis on the beach is no sure sign of the acceptance of the human body. Certainly, the sight of naked feminine beauty at that fleeting stage when adolescence has just passed into maturity should give pleasure. But this, if healthy, should be a part, a relatively small part, of the full acceptance of the bodily reality of people, an acceptance with delight, but also, if total, necessarily with compassion and understanding tenderness. To isolate an ideal moment of feminine physical beauty is precisely to abstract. What is then presented as a result of that mental reduction of bodily reality is not a person in the flesh, not even a stranger, not really a human body, but an abstract form, used as device in the solitary fantasies and selfish purposes of an isolated, unrelated self. To accept the human body, or better, the bodily reality and presence of human persons, is to respond positively to bodies as humanly expressive even when they do not have a perfect physical form. I think of the artist, Frederick Franck, who meditatively draws the naked bodies of people of different ages and shapes.[4] If a husband and wife truly relate to each other, they will know and love each other's body as bearing the marks of the pain, the struggle, the accidents of life; as showing the gradual signs of aging; as evoking care as well as pleasure, though the two are not exclusive in the outgoing joy of love.

The bodily beauty of men and women, the beauty that shines forth physically, is not purely physical. Everyone will admit this in regard to the human face. Facial beauty insofar as it comes from perfect physical proportions, firm flesh, and finely textured skin, can of itself be dead and unattractive. Indeed, such features may be the basis of an ugly countenance, expressing a selfish or hateful personality. But a face can have a quite extraordinary beauty in the mobile expressiveness with which it presents a rich, lovable personality, despite features in themselves physically ugly. The same is true of the body as a whole. Its living beauty is never exclusively physical.

> . . . the spouse, the bride
> Is never naked. A fictive covering
> Weaves always glistening from the heart and mind.[5]

Clothes, however, do allow levels of expressiveness. They cover the body, and thus they create a reserve of communicatory power for intimate relationships. They amplify the body language of bearing and gesture, stance and movement. People who wear stiff clothes have stiff bodies, or are suffering under convention. New ways of living in the body bring new forms of clothing. Nudity may thus be a rejection of the human body, an attempt to deny or destroy its human expressiveness. It turns the human person, the "illimitable spheres of you" into monotonous, nameless earth.[6] It reduces the sensuously spiritual to the pure physicality of the sensual.

It would be a mistake to interpret the sensuality of our day as an acceptance of the body. When women, at great discomfort, force their bodies to conform to an ideal of young and changeless beauty, they are denying the reality of their actual bodies. Men who engage in fantasies of sexual athletics, and perhaps even try to live them out, are refusing their sexuality as an organic, living and aging, bodily power and are conceiving it as a machine. *La Sexe machine* is the apt name of a Montreal topless nightclub. Sensuality is a rejection of the body, because in sensual indulgence the body is driven by the mind against its own spontaneous rhythms.

The rejection of matter, in particular of the living matter of the body, is characteristic of our culture today. If we ignore marginal groups and some recently emergent trends, we can say that people in general have no feel or appreciation for the texture of material things.

Processed food is a reduction of the materiality of food. I came across an absurd illustration of that in an advertisement for grapefruit tablets. Directed to those on a slimming diet requiring the consumption of large quantities of grapefruit, it proclaimed the advantage of getting the goodness of grapefruit without the messiness of handling the actual fruit. That line of sales talk presupposes a public indifferent to the succulence of fruit. Various tasty species of apple, I am told, are no longer marketed, because people will only buy apples with shiny, unmarked skin and those varieties are dull and spotted by nature. And so we all must have less tasty varieties coated with paraffin. Much more could be said; but let bread, because of its eucharistic association, stand as the supreme example. What passes for bread in North America is almost completely lacking in the qualities we delight in when we love matter.

There is a cluster of problems connected with the decline in the quality of food—problems, for instance, of mass production and distribution. I am not trying to explain the whole situation as a revulsion from matter. But whether as a consequence or as a cause of other factors, there is a retreat from matter and its qualities in the modern handling of food. Processing and packaging, additives, and refrigeration: all are attempts to conquer the natural propensity of matter to change and decay. Success in this is achieved only by destroying many of the material qualities of the product. I am not concerned with the rights and wrongs of doing that. Clearly, much of it is necessary. I want to insist, however, that it does not represent an attachment to matter, a love and appreciation of material qualities, but, on the contrary, a brutal subjection of matter to the mind. And in some people it has caused a dislike of the rich, organic texture of unprocessed foods and an unhealthy fear of decay.

The same analysis applies to other features of the modern scene. People speak of the concrete wilderness of our cities. But it would be truer to speak of them as wilderness of the unfeeling mind. A modern city is not a material environment but a cerebral nightmare. It is the result of ignoring all sensuous factors and using materials in as abstract a way as possible, so as to make an environment which approaches the formal purity of a mental projection. The men who create modern cities are, it would seem, lost in the wilderness of the mind when cut off from feeling. Men with a rich, integrated sensuousness could not have made the present urban environment. At most, one would credit them with some uncoordinated feelings on the periphery of their lives. Hence they think they are satisfying sensuous needs when they add a few decorative trimmings.

To call our age materialistic is a false interpretation. The dominant culture of our time has no love or appreciation of matter, no feel for it, especially not for living matter with its organic rhythms, its processes of growth and decay. Plastic flowers may serve as a typical symbol. Plastic flowers spring, not from the earth, but from man's head. They are a denial of the fragile beauty of flowers, which is inseparable from decay and death. To want to prevent a daffodil from fading, to try to cancel its temporal rhythm, is to have seen but not felt its beauty. Plastic flowers were created, not by feeling or sensuous enjoyment, but by the mind.

And the mind invented money. Money is material wealth made abstract, made immaterial. The pursuit of money is a mental, not a material, pursuit. A man in touch with the sensuous rhythms of his body would undoubtedly be a disabled contender in the race to accumulate money.

Perhaps we could most accurately call our age the machine age. The machine is matter when overcome and subordinated to the mind. To make a machine is to subdue matter's own rhythms and processes and subject them to mentally devised rhythms and processes. And sensuality, as I have remarked, is the reduction of the human body to a machine.

I want to introduce a distinction here between sensuousness and sensuality. Sensuousness is when we participate in the spontaneous rhythms and responses of the body and are open to the joys and delights, the pain, suffering, and stress of bodily experience. It implies an ability to relax, which I understand as allowing the spontaneous responsiveness of the body to hold sway and suspending the controlling and driving impetus of the rational mind and will. Sensuality, in contrast, is what happens when the body is driven by the mind and used as an instrument of pleasure for reasons found in man's mental and spiritual state. The roots of sensuality are not in bodily impulses, but in man's mind. As John Wren-Lewis writes:

> . . . *the body itself seems to know that it does not want sensual indulgence.* It takes only a small amount of real sensory awareness to awaken the body to the fact that it is being biologically maltreated by the way the mind organises life, and this maltreatment happens as much when the individual wallows in self-indulgent sensuality as it does when he strives neurotically for wealth and power, regiments himself to mechanical work-routines or suffers extreme poverty.[7]

Sensuality is the submission of the body to the driving, straining consciousness of a mind alienated from its bodiliness. It is not, despite the traditional view, the subjection of the mind to bodily impulses. In sensuality the body does not enslave; it is enslaved.

I would further argue that sensuousness accompanies a sacramental, mystical view of the world, in which the body and physical nature are mediatory of the spirit, whereas sensuality implies a destruction of the mediatory, symbolic character of the physical world and the reduction of that world to pure physicality.

There are, I think, two different ways of relating to the physical world, including our own bodies.

The first is when human consciousness and physical reality are bound together in a relation of mutual participation. Neither is experienced or conceived without the other. Physical phenomena are then apprehended, not as bare facts, but as representations full of human meanings. They are taken as expressions of man's conscious life, extensions and counterparts of this experience as subject. Interpreted by human consciousness, they also serve as hierophanies or manifestations of the holy, transcendent reality in which they participate. Further, they enter into the dynamism of man's spirit, not only as sacred objects, but as embodiments of the eros in him as subject toward the mystery of that same transcendent reality. Physical phenomena are thus symbols, but not in the sense of having a subjective meaning superimposed upon a literal, factual reality, alone regarded as objective. They are apprehended in their very consistency and reality as expressive of the consciousness present in man and of the mystery present in the universe. They are expressive of both because participating in both.

In the context of that relationship with the physical world, bodily sensuous experience becomes a vehicle of the mystical. The spontaneity of the body becomes the outward form and perceptible presence of the spontaneity of the spirit. Sensuous eros becomes penetrated with spiritual affectivity. In other words, what is here called sensuousness is feeling as I have analyzed it, but now seen and named from the bodily side of the total response.

One may, however, relate to the physical world in a second way; that is, by reducing it to physical facts. The phenomena of sense experience are then made into physical objects and events, seen as independent of the consciousness of the observer and thus deprived of any meaning other than their physical relationships. Physical objects are put apart from conscious subjects and reduced to a physicality stripped of any further meaning. Such a world is no longer sacramental; it no longer mediates the mystical.

When such a mode of relating to the physical world is not restricted to limited intellectual and technical contexts, but made the framework for human living, it has sensuality as its counterpart. Sensuality arises when the body is objectified as a physical object to be used and is thus stripped of its sacramental meaning and mystical associations.

The use of the word "body" in reference to our own bodily reality, though unavoidable without clumsiness, may imply the reduction of the body to a physical object. We should do better to speak of "bodiliness" when referring to our personal experience as embodied subjects. When we say "body" we objectify, and the danger is that we objectify our bodiliness only partially, as though it were merely physical and not the embodiment of spirit. We might almost say that "bodiliness" is what we experience when we live sensuously as embodied persons; but "the body" is what we experience when we indulge in sensuality and relate to our own bodies as physical objects alienated from us.

Both the world as sacramental and the world as reduced to its pure physicality result from the constructive activity of human consciousness. It is a common mistake to suppose that the world, when taken as merely physical, is the real world, objectively out there somehow, the literally true; and that the world as sacramental and as mediating mystical experience is less real. But both worlds arise from an interaction with realities independent of man, and each world depends upon a particular mode of human apprehension and a constructive ordering or world-making activity by man. The difference is that the world as sacramental is the world as apprehended through that total response I have analyzed as feeling, and the world as purely physical is apprehended by that partial, limited response we call intellectual. Further, the world as sacramental is constructed through the poetic, imaginative, sensuous faculties of men, and the world as purely physical is the product of reason in its abstract, mathematical, and logical functioning.

Sensuality is a subordination of the body to the calculating mind. It implies a denial of the participatory mode of relating to the body and physical world, an ignoring or rejection of the sacramental meaning and mystical mediation of bodiliness. It is basically a rejection of the body, a rejection of its spontaneous rhythms, of its expressiveness, of its eros—which is an eros toward transcendent values.

The puritan, then, who sees the body merely as a sensual obstacle to the moral and religious life, and the libertine who sees the body as a mere instrument of pleasure, have the same conception of the human body and the same attitude to it. Both, in fact, reject bodiliness. Both fear and repudiate the spontaneous, sensuous eros of the body. Both ignore or deny its sacramental meaning and mystical mediation. Both reduce the body to its pure physicality and set it over against a rational consciousness alienated from the body. Both shut their inner self off from feeling as the spontaneous, connatural response to values, because they fear its independence of the controlling consciousness of the rational self, its transcendence of established rules and conventions, and its frequent disruption of preconceived and calculated goals.

But why has the religious consciousness so commonly rejected the body? Why has it refused sensuousness and regarded the spontaneous rhythms and responses of the body as obstacles to the spirit? It has engaged in a punitive ascetic discipline that negates the body and endeavors to mortify or deaden its affectivity. Bodiliness is not seen as mediating but as blocking that "blind stirring of love"—as *The Cloud of Unknowing* calls it—that movement toward mystery which is the primary element in religious experience.

There are a number of different factors operative here. No single factor provides an adequate explanation. For example: Much religion is neurotic inasmuch as it serves the devious purposes of a divided or enclosed self. A neurosis has been caused by some trauma or lesser flaw in development. The neurotic self avoids reality and protects itself by constructing an unreal world. Genuine feeling, with its sense of reality, would cause a painful collapse of that precarious structure. The neurotic, therefore, wards off feeling. This can be done by embracing a harsh, puritanical religious outlook. Religion of that kind offers an alternative to sensuality, which is also a refusal of feeling but in a different mode. Sometimes both solutions are tried, either successively or in a guilt-ridden oscillation. Another example: the routinization of religion into established forms creates a fear of spontaneity in the many who prefer security to freedom; it is easier to reject the spontaneity of sensuousness or embodied spirit on speciously religious grounds than openly to reject the spirit. Again, the widespread religious refusal of the body has been caused in part by the impact, both open and covert, of various forms of doctrinal dualism directly rejecting the body or matter or sex as evil.

I am not, then, claiming that the following line of analysis is either exclusive or exhaustive. I am selecting some considerations that seem to me to speak to people with a traditional Christian background who are trying to achieve a positive relationship between bodiliness and the life of the spirit. My suggestion is that a powerful factor in the religious fear and repudiation of sensuousness is a partly wrong interpretation of the present disorder of human existence. Somehow mankind has gone wrong, and in a way that affects every individual born into this world. A first innocence of human living is no longer available, at least as a stable state. Everyone has to struggle through to a second innocence, and to do that demands repentance, conversion, and being born again.

We meet here the contrast made so eloquently by William James in his chapters on "The Religion of Healthy-Mindedness" and "The Sick Soul."[8] He borrowed and made famous a distinction from Francis Newman between the once-born and the twice-born. The healthy-minded are those who need to be born only once. For them, the once-born, happiness is congenital and irreclaimable. They look on all things and see that they are good and have an inability to feel evil. Sick souls, on the contrary, must be twice-born in order to be happy. They are persuaded that "evil aspects of our life are of its very essence, and that the world's meaning most comes home to us when we lay them most to heart."[9]

William James himself was more concerned with describing than with evaluating the two. Further, he recognized that in their extreme form they are abstract types; in the concrete, we meet intermediate varieties and mixtures. Since, however, my present plea for sensuousness supports some features of the healthy-minded religion of the once-born, I want to insist here that, taken as a whole, I regard it as inadequate to human experience. First innocence, I repeat, is unavailable. It has its image in the passing, springlike periods that youth or one of the fresh beginnings of life may bring. But it is not itself a reality. Those who live as though it were are blind to themselves and others, and often make one shudder at the unfeeling clumsiness of their far from innocent self-ishness.

We cannot, therefore, relax without turmoil into a sensuous spontaneity, where all will be sweetness and light. We have to confront the disorder of the race into which we were born, together with our own involvement in that disorder, and seek a remedy. We have to be converted and born again. We are called to repentance and forgiveness.

Religions differ widely in the analysis and explanation they give of human disorder. We find a universal, minimum agreement that, in the words of John Wren-Lewis, "there is, and has always been a potentiality in human beings for something very much more than the ordinary levels of life which mankind has managed to achieve in any society in history."[10] Christianity, as is well known, goes beyond that minimum recognition of human dissatisfaction and frustration by speaking of sin.

Sin is not just the sense of unrealized potentiality; it means more than the difficulties attendant upon growth. Those who appeal to sin to explain human disorder are not content to understand, with the Hindus and Buddhists, that disorder as due to a simple mistake; in other words, as the result of an error or illusion concerning the world and the individual self and their relation to reality. Human frustration is not sin, but the result of sin. Whatever illusions and errors may blind men are not themselves sin, but the results of sin. Sin is located right in the higher potentialities of man. Sin means—to quote John Wren-Lewis again—that *"human beings have voluntarily used those higher potentialities to create false ways of living in which the higher potentialities are denied."*[11]

This is expressed in theistic imagery by speaking of sin as an offence against God, because for theism the higher potentialities of man lie in his relationship with God. But the abstract formulation is more useful here. It drives home the truth that the roots of human disorder are in man's higher potentialities. The basic disorder is an abuse of those higher powers: man has blocked their inherent dynamism toward the transcendent and twisted them back to serve the purposes of an egocentric self.

That analysis corresponds to the traditional Christian understanding of the sickness or disorder of the human condition. Christians have always denied in theory that the greater sins are the sins of the flesh. Such sins are sins of weakness; the darker evil lies in sins of the spirit. Again, the primordial sin, whether of the race or of the individual, has always been identified as pride or disobedience, not lust. There should therefore be no question of attributing any view to Christianity which would find the roots of human disorder in man's physical organism and would consequently reject sensuous experience as in itself evil.

Nevertheless, at this point the traditional Christian analysis of the human condition took, in my opinion, a wrong turning, which resulted in a rejection of sensuousness, a negative, punitive asceticism, and an infiltration of dualistic elements into Christian teaching and practice.

The paradigm most frequently used for sin was the rebellion of man against the authority and rule of God. This fitted in with theism, but it also corresponded to an hierarchical view of the cosmos, in which everything was ordered according to higher and lower degrees, with the higher governing the lower and the lower being subject to the higher. Human nature with its complex makeup of higher and lower powers was similarly conceived and inserted into the cosmic scheme. Sin was interpreted as the introduction of anarchy into this hierarchical order. Man refused to submit to the authority of God. The inevitable consequence was that he himself lost his authority over his own nature. The anarchy within man himself was then understood as the loss of rational control by the mind and will over the physical organism and the movements of sense appetite. The entire relationship to bodiliness came to be seen in terms of a sinful rebellion of the bodily appetites against the control of reason and will. It was a rebellion that enslaved sinners to the body and demanded a continuous struggle on the part of the converted to bring the body, with its desires and passions, under control. Rational control meant, in effect, the mortification or deadening of all bodily desires and affections of those striving for holiness or engaged in the mystical way, because no one seeking union with God would, it was thought, voluntarily arouse an affectivity for sense objects or the things of this world.

The result was a model of human nature which exaggerated the role of purposive mind and of deliberate, voluntary decision. Sensuous spontaneity was feared and denigrated as a disorder consequent upon sin and the sign of sinfulness. This left little room for feeling as a spontaneous, connatural, and total response of the embodied person. Even religious feelings became suspect as escaping from the prior deliberate control of the will.

Something of that model may be found in Paul. He writes, in Romans 7:21-25:

> So I find it to be a law that when I want to do right, evil lies close at hand. For I delight in the law of God, in my inmost self, but I see in my members another law at war with the law of my mind and making me captive to the law of sin which dwells in my members. Wretched man that I am! Who will deliver me from this body of death? Thanks be to God through Jesus Christ our Lord! So then, I of myself serve the law of God with my mind, but with my flesh I serve the law of sin.

Paul, with his borrowings here from Greek thought, has the human condition wrong, I venture to suggest. The law of sin does not dwell in the bodily members, keeping the mind back from God. A much sounder analysis is that the law of sin dwells in the mind, which drives the bodily members to its sinful purposes, blocking their own inherent spontaneity and responsiveness. Freed from the sinful law of the mind, the bodily members would mediate the spirit.

Augustine, however, gave the classic presentation of the model, according to which in sinful man the bodily appetites are in rebellion against control by reason and will. A striking instance of his teaching, which was made known to a wider public by C. S. Lewis in *A Preface to Paradise Lost*,[12] is found in *The City of God,* Book XIV, chapters 15 and following. After stating that the just punishment of man's disobedience to God was the disobedience of the flesh to the will, he then applies this principle to the will's control or lack of control over the genital organs. Before the Fall, according to Augustine, Adam and Eve had their genital organs directly under the control of their wills, as we even now have such control over our hands, feet, and fingers. That is why they were unashamed in their nakedness. Had they not sinned, they would have come together with their generative organs moved by will only and "without the exorbitance of hotter desire."[13] Children thus would have been generated by quiet will, not as now by headlong lust.[14] It is the present lack of control over the genital organs that makes the sexual act an instance of shameful lust even in marriage. The wise and godly man would "rather (if he could) beget his children without his lust, that his members might obey his mind in this act of propagation, as his other members in fulfilling their particular functions, and be ruled by his will, not compelled by concupiscence."[15]

The desire to eradicate all spontaneous sexual movements and make sexual activity a matter of cool, deliberate will is so grotesque that it provides the *reductio ad absurdum* of the whole idea that man's bodily appetites and responses should function only under the direct control of the will. (Augustine, we may add, was so anxious for voluntary control of the body that he even said our first parents were never "unwillingly sleepy".)[16] But it is worth noting that Augustine's ideal is an ideal shared by all those given over to sensuality. He himself observes that "the lovers of these carnal delights themselves cannot have this emotion at their will,"[17] but this does not provoke him to reflect that he and they have the same desire to bring sexual spontaneity under control.

I am reminded here of that masterly portrayal of libertinism, the novel *Les Liaisons dangereuses* by Pierre Choderlos de Laclos. Both the Vicomte de Valmont and the Marquise de Merteuil, the two chief characters whose sexual intrigues and exploits the book recounts, have in common as the principal trait of each their determination to remain in complete control of each situation, of their own lives, and of the lives of other people. The ability to dominate both themselves and others is for them the supreme value. They regard any spontaneous movements of tenderness and love as weaknesses to be guarded against. Martin Turnell writes:

> Love is usually regarded as an emotional experience in which sexual passion is one of the factors. Now the thought that they can for a single moment be at the mercy of their emotions, or of what Valmont acrimoniously calls *cette passion pusillanime,* is intolerable both to him and to Mme de Merteuil. Their aim is to eliminate the emotional factor altogether. Love comes to mean the intellectual satisfaction they get from the pursuit and defeat of the "enemy," and the sensual pleasure which accompanies it.[18]

Something similar is true of all sensualists. Not all have the power of rational control of Laclos's characters, but all would like to have their sexual faculties under the direct control of their will, so as to use them just as they decide for their calculated purposes.

I contend that we should reject any model of human nature that divides man, even in his present sinful condition, into two levels or sets of powers, with the mind and will as the dwelling place of spirit and the body as the locus of sin. Bodily spontaneity should not be seen as a law of sin, warring against a mind and will united to God; nor should the aim of ascetic discipline be the bringing of bodily desires, emotions, and movements under the direct control of the rational will. The sinful disorder in man is not a disorder that divides one part of man—the body—against another part of man—the rational faculties. It is a disorder that divides the whole of man against himself. The higher powers of man are turned back against themselves, their inner dynamism frustrated; and the lower powers, since they form a unity with the higher as their embodiment, are thereby twisted out of their own inherent tendency. Bodiliness, instead of mediating the movement of a self open to the mysterious transcendent, becomes the arena in which the restless, permanent dissatisfaction of a self-enclosed ego works itself out in drives of gluttony and lust or, alternatively, in excesses of punitive discipline.

Complete rational control over the body is not an ideal. To make it so would be to reject the body and the spirit. A rejection of the body would be implied, because it is the very nature of bodily sensitivity to respond immediately and spontaneously to its appropriate objects. There is no disorder in responding sensuously to what meets us in the flow of sense experience. The disorder lies in the lust to possess for ourselves all we meet; in other words, in turning sensuousness into sensuality by subordinating it to the narrow purposes of an egocentric self.

The ideal of complete rational control also rejects the spirit, because the spirit is present in spontaneity. Where there is spontaneity, the person is receptive, no longer enclosed within the boundaries of the individual ego. Allowing spontaneity means being receptive; being responsive to the world in which we live and to other persons; exposing ourselves to the life around us, to the joy, delight, pain, sorrow, enthusiasm, indignation, compassion, and love it provokes; and letting ourselves be led against the conventions of established society to respond to the truth of a particular situation. Sensuousness is the embodiment of the spirit's spontaneity. To eradicate sensuous spontaneity would be, for us as bodily persons, to block the spirit.

What is wanted, therefore, is an attitude of fundamental trust in the body, a recognition that if we can recover its genuine spontaneity, its rhythms and responses, it will become a medium of spiritual salvation. To rediscover bodiliness will be to rediscover our openness to reality. If we can genuinely feel, we will break out of our imprisoned egos and be one with the world and with God. I recall here the description of Anna in Morley Callaghan's novel *They Shall Inherit the Earth:*

> She went on from day to day, living and loving and exposing the fulness and wholeness of herself to the life around her. If to be poor in spirit meant to be without false pride, to be humble enough to forget oneself, then she was poor in spirit, for she gave herself to everything that touched her, she let herself be, she lost herself in the fulness of the world, and in losing herself she found the world, and she possessed her own soul. People like her could have everything. They could inherit the earth.[19]

Not a denial of the world, but an openness to it is what our sinful egos need. Shrunk within the insulated cell of their selfishness, they must be taught how to feel, not how to deny feeling.

On that basis I want to distinguish between two kinds of asceticism, which I shall call the asceticism of punitive discipline and the asceticism of achieved spontaneity. Most traditional Christian asceticism is of the first kind.

The word "mortification" well expresses the aim, namely, the deadening of all bodily impulses and of all affectivity, particularly sensuous, directed to the things and persons of this world. I have already given reasons why I regard that aim as ill-conceived. Sensuality may be opaque, but sensuousness is transparent with the spirit. The body is the patterning of spirit. Those who strive for a pure immateriality of response to God are not seeking him from the center of their being, but from the neurotic circle of an ego alienated from its bodiliness and, consequently, from the world and other people.

The adjective "punitive" indicates the essential trait of the method. This is the application to oneself of the same policy of punishment or, to use the psychological jargon, of negative reinforcement, which for so long dominated the education of children. Hence the line of criticism is the same. All that has been said about the counterproductive effects and even serious harmfulness of punishment as a method of education for children is equally true of traditional asceticism. The method produces unhealthy distortions of behavior. Its usual result is to strengthen the mental condition that originally caused the imperious impulses one is trying to correct and control.

Granted there is an unavoidable penal element in human life as it is at present. But this does not consist in any need to impose punishment as a discipline upon oneself or on others. It consists in the negative consequences—the harm and destruction, the pain and suffering—sinful actions of themselves bring down upon their doers and others. We have to accept those consequences, not deny or dismiss them, when we acknowledge our sins. Repentance implies a willingness to work conscientiously through them and their demands, so that they become a means of transformation. We can thus speak of the penal consequences of sin becoming means of redemption. But a policy of punitive asceticism, far from facilitating the process of transformation, is more likely to reinforce the destructive effects of sin. And while it may be noble voluntarily to enter into the situation of others and accept the consequences of doing so, it is morbid to punish ourselves for the deeds of others.

The second kind of asceticism was suggested to me by Zen and by the various movements today promoting sensory awareness. The aim is positive: bodily spontaneity, the recovery of the rhythms and responses of the body, the release of feeling, the development of feeling responses to the world and other people, the awakening of such sensory awareness as will prevent the misuse of the body by the mind in sensuality, power-seeking and money-making. The methods are many and various.[20] It will take some time to sort the wheat from the chaff in all that is advocated and practiced today. But if we resist the mental drive to be up with the latest trends and, instead, learn to find and trust our own genuine feelings, we shall begin to discriminate.

In regard to the bodily rhythms directly supporting prayer, those who remain within the Christian tradition are being chiefly influenced by Zen. Many Christians have recognized the truth of what William Johnston remarks in his book, *Christian Zen:* "For the fact is that Western prayer is not sufficiently visceral—it is preoccupied with the brain and not with the deeper layers of the body where the power to approach the spiritual is generated."[21] He also says: "There is a basic rhythm in the body, linked to a consciousness that is deeper than is ordinarily experienced . . . anyone who wants to meditate in depth must find this rhythm and the consciousness that accompanies it."[22] I will not repeat here what he says concerning the various ways to reach that rhythm. But I do want to comment on the story he told in the first chapter. He had been attending a Zen temple to sit in meditation. After a time the priest in charge of the temple called him aside, thanked him for coming, and then

said that he would like to see a Christian monastery.
Johnston recalls his embarrassment: "I felt that there was
not in Tokyo a Christian monastery to which I could
introduce him with reasonable hope that he would be
edified."[23] Anyone with some knowledge of the average
male religious house at once realizes what he means.
What is wrong is not just a neglect of contemplation, but
an utter lack of sensitivity to the bodily and material
environment. The monasteries are indeed "so much like
offices";[24] there is an absence of what I have called sensuousness, needed to make all the material surroundings
vibrant with the spirit.

   Discipline, demanding discipline, is required by the
second kind of asceticism. Nevertheless, I have called it
the asceticism of achieved spontaneity. That might seem
to be a contradiction, but experience shows that it is not
so. The pianist, for example, knows that the technically
learnable part of his art has to be practiced to the satura-
tion level. The aim, however, is not to acquire a deliberate, rational control of his playing. On the contrary, it is
done to reach the point where there is no further need of
a controlling intelligence. But playing the piano is not an
automatism, and no merely mechanical dexterity will
produce art. When a high level of technical accomplish-
ment has been attained, there can be, and for art there
must be, a breakthrough to a new spontaneity in which
the player responds to the music through his fingers and
the piano with an immediacy of feeling. Because of his
technical skill, the player is able to respond connaturally
and spontaneously in his art, in a manner analogous to
our everyday responses, but on a different level. He
achieves an artless art. An excellent account of such
achieved spontaneity is given by Eugen Herrigel in his
well-known book, *Zen in the Art of Archery*.[25]

   I believe the same principle applies to the whole
range of feelings, including affective responses to other
people and to moral and religious values. An appeal to

spontaneity is not a license for, in T. S. Eliot's phrase, "undisciplined squads of emotion."[26] There is a spontaneity that comes only through discipline, but it is a positive discipline with a respect for bodiliness, not a discipline that negates the body as a medium of spirit.

Some will be disturbed by the stress upon technique. The elaborate techniques of traditional asceticism in its heyday are forgotten. All the same, it was always taught that the ascetic practices were only a means, not an end. They could not replace sincere repentance of heart or a genuine love of God. Perhaps it is necessary to state that the same holds good of a positive approach to bodiliness: mere technique is not enough. Those who, like myself, do not believe that a first innocence is available, and who insist that we must all be born again, cannot suppose that techniques of sensory awareness—yoga, Zen methods of concentration and of artless art, and so on—will of themselves suffice. The cultivation of sensory awareness to offset the deleterious effects of a mode of life—say pursuit of money or power, which one has no intention of relinquishing—is a sham. The new asceticism, like the old, is meaningless unless it carries with it a transformation of conscious life, repentance, and conversion. On the other hand, at least as much must be allowed to the new techniques as to the old; namely, that if pursued they will mediate that transforming conversion. A breakthrough to genuine sensory awareness may not be the end, but it does form a beginning. If people would stop maltreating their bodies as machines for their egocentric purposes, they might be drawn to take the first steps in the mystical ascent.

This brings me back, in concluding this chapter, to John of the Cross, with whom I began. If one reads him through carefully, one finds that he is primarily concerned with detachment. The negative asceticism is incidental to that, largely explicable as cultural baggage. His insistence upon the absolute necessity of detachment is similar to that found in Zen. For both, attachment to anything whatsoever is the enemy that blocks progress in contemplation. I myself, then, would readily grant that detachment is the condition we must aim at if we are serious in the mystical quest. But detachment may be interpreted in two different ways. The first is to take it as the eradication or deadening of all affectivity, especially sensuous. The second is to see it as the retrieval of the self-transcending, self-forgetting dynamism of all human, sensuous affectivity when no longer dominated by the ego. Sensuousness is essentially mediatory of spirit; its own dynamism is not the cause of attachment, which is the attempt of an enclosed ego to fill its emptiness. Far from resulting from sensuous affection, attachment blunts and destroys it.

Clearly, I am defending the second interpretation of detachment. My next step, therefore, must be to examine the question of the self.

III.
From the Interior Self to the Isolated Ego

If the purpose of asceticism is detachment, the asceticism of punitive discipline is counterproductive because it intensifies egocentric consciousness. Its policy of negative discipline to bring bodily desires and impulses under control presupposes and deepens a division in the person between a controlling rational consciousness, the ego, and the rest of human makeup, the me, which is made the object of control. Everything in man, except the narrow circle of an ego-consciousness contracted to a rational, deliberating, decisional power, is placed with nature as a thing to be mastered. There is a quasi-detachment from nature and the body, but it is an alienation, not a true detachment. Such alienation is correlative to a high degree of egocentricity. The result is the very opposite of self-transcendence, which presupposes an expansion, not a contraction, of consciousness; a relation of participation in nature, not alienation from it; a spontaneity of response to reality, not a deliberate, rational control by the ego of every moment.

Who is to control the controller? That is the question which renders nugatory any attempt to find the solution to the disorder in human life in self-control. The core of the disorder lies in the self. The self has to be healed; its attempt to control the universe is the sickness to be cured, not a source of remedy. The inmost or interior self, the wellspring of centered acts of the total person, and thus of religious feeling, is not to be identified with the rationally conscious ego, which by its deliberations and decisions exercises control over ordinary activities in this world.

That is undoubtedly so for the Asian religions. In the Indian tradition the system of Advaita Vedānta, the form of Hindu thought most widely known in the West, identifies the *ātman* or deepest self with Brahman, the ultimate reality of the cosmos, and thus places its reality beyond the plurality or individual egos. But even outside the strict monism of Advaita Vedānta, a distinction between the empirical self and the inner self is common to the various Hindu schools and sects.

Theravāda Buddhism maintains that there is no permanent self underlying the psychological and physical events making up the individual. This denial is not merely a denial of a permanent empirical self, but also, in the doctrine of *anātta,* a denial of any eternal self. Clearly, therefore, the movement of religious experience or thrust for nirvana in this form of Buddhism is toward a complete transcendence of the rational, controlling self or ego-consciousness. In Mahāyāna Buddhism, the realization of Buddhahood is the entry into a unity beyond the multiplicity of individual selves. The Buddha nature is one in all.

Zen proclaims an insight beyond subject and object, a liberation from the limitations of the individual ego and a discovery of one's original nature beyond the empirical self. Herrigel writes of Zen enlightenment:

With this rebirth the enlightened at once become aware of what they are in the ground of their being: they perceive their Buddha nature. Yet it would be contrary to the facts of experience to call this nature the "better self" or "real ego," or even the "super-ego." In this "primary sphere" there is nothing like an ego or self any more. This original nature is, rather, the selfless and egoless Ground, the nameless and formless root of the self.[1]

That quotation makes explicit the questions raised by the Asian tradition as a whole. In the last analysis, is there identity or duality between the inmost self and ultimate reality? Is religious experience a movement beyond any plurality of selves to a oneness without distinction in the absolute? Is mystical experience an experience of identity with the ground of being or of loving union with God? All such questions concern the nature of the interior self. They will have to be considered later. The point to be made at the moment is that the seat of religious experience is not the rationally conscious ego, nor does that ego have the primary role in achieving enlightenment or liberation.

The Christian tradition, because of its theism and its stress upon the divine transcendence, is antipathetic to any monism and insists upon the distinction between the inmost self and God, even in the highest reaches of the mystical ascent and in the full achievement of salvation. Again, for reasons to be discussed shortly, it has been marked by an emphasis upon the individual. Nevertheless, even in the Christian tradition, the interior self, the place of religious experience, is beyond the ego, and is sometimes spoken of in terms of identity with God or the Spirit.

These passages from Paul declare a union with Christ by the Spirit so close that Christ or the Spirit is said to be the true subject of our new life and prayer as sons of God:

... it is no longer I who live, but Christ who lives in me
(Gal. 2:20); And because you are sons, God has sent the
Spirit of his Son into our hearts, crying, "Abba! Father!"
(Gal. 4:6); When we cry, "Abba! Father!" it is the Spirit
himself bearing witness with our spirit that we are children of God (Rom. 8:15, 16); Likewise the Spirit helps us
in our weakness; for we do not know how to pray as we
ought, but the Spirit himself intercedes for us with sighs
too deep for words. And he who searches the hearts of
men knows what is the mind of the Spirit, because the
Spirit intercedes for the saints according to the will of
God (Rom. 8:26, 27).

These statements, together with similar statements
elsewhere in the New Testament, notably in John, have
been taken up in the theology of grace. There, in systematic fashion, it has been argued that we become sons
of God, capable of a new, supernatural life, by the indwelling of the Spirit, united to us, so that his presence
transforms our nature, raising it to a new level of being
and action. Only as one with the indwelling Spirit are we
able to perform actions proper to our state as sons of
God. Therefore, the principle or subject of our new life is
not ourselves, even if helped in some fashion from without by God's grace, but ourselves as one with the Spirit, as
being new selves or new beings in and through his abid-
ing presence. For that reason, God is not just the object of
our worship and love, but is within us as the subjective
principle of that love and worship.

If we turn from the theological to the Christian
mystical tradition, we find that this also speaks of an
interior self beyond the ego and, further, uses the language of identity of the relation of this self to God.
Christian mystics refer to "the depth of the soul," "the
fine point of the soul," "the substance of the soul," "the
deepest center of the soul," and so forth, as the place of
union with God. John of the Cross, for example, in *Living
Flame of Love*, begins the first stanza with the words, "Oh,
living flame of love/ That tenderly woundest my soul in
its deepest centre," and in his commentary he writes:

For this feast of the Holy Spirit takes place in the substance of the soul, where neither the devil nor the world nor sense can enter; and therefore the more interior it is, the more is it secure, substantial and delectable; for the more interior it is the purer is it, and the more of purity there is in it, the more abundantly and frequently and widely does God communicate Himself.

A little later he says:

The centre of the soul is God; and, when the soul has attained to Him according to the whole capacity of its being, and according to the force of its operation, it will have reached the last and the deep centre of the soul, which will be when with all its powers it loves and understands and enjoys God . . .[2]

But it is the earlier writer, Meister Eckhart, whose expressions of identity between the inmost self and God are the boldest and the most reminiscent of the Asian tradition. Thus he writes:

What the eternal Father teaches is his own Being, Nature, and Godhead—which he is always revealing through his only begotten Son. He teaches that we are to be identical with him. To deny one's self is to be the only begotten Son of God and one who does so has for himself all the properties of that Son.

And again, in a famous passage:

The eye by which I see God is the same as the eye by which God sees me. My eye and God's eye are one and the same—one in seeing, one in knowing, and one in loving.[3]

Thomas Merton puts Christian mysticism alongside the mysticism of other religions as implying a subject beyond any individual ego:

. . . it is basic to Zen, to Sufism and to Christian mysticism (to mention only those approaches to transcendent experience with which the writer is familiar) *to radically and*

unconditionally question the ego which appears to be the subject
of the transcendent experience, and thus of course to radically
question the whole nature of the experience itself precisely as "experience."[4]

Christians, therefore, are not being true to the rich
depths of their own tradition when they suppose that
religious experience can be presented as the human person in his individual ego-consciousness loving God as
object. Though in a way peculiar to itself, the Christian
tradition, like the Asian religious traditions, raises questions concerning the reality and value of the self.

Before considering the particular development of
the problematic of the self in the West, however, I want to
offer some psychological and philosophical reflections
concerning the self. To do this will, I hope, help to give
point to the historical remarks.

The individual self begins as a potentiality, and there
is a long and complex process of growth and development before the self emerges in its individuality and
becomes fully operative as a conscious subject and agent.
The consciousness proper to the self as subject is the
presence of the self to itself in those operations, such as
sense perception, activities of intelligence, free and responsible actions, which of their nature imply a subjective
as well as an objective awareness. In other words, consciousness is the self-awareness intrinsic in all those actions we call conscious. In such actions the attention may
be wholly concentrated upon the object, as when a music-
lover is enraptured by a symphony or a mathematician
is absorbed in a problem; and yet there is always that self-
presence of the subject which distinguishes those actions
as conscious from unconscious levels of operation.

The self-awareness intrinsic to conscious operations
should be distinguished from the reflexive self-
awareness resulting from the turning back of the subject
upon itself in introspection when it makes itself the object
of its attention. That reflexive kind of self-consciousness

presupposes the original, intrinsic subjectivity or self-presence in conscious acts themselves, where the object on which attention is focused may be other than the subject. Without such immediate consciousness, there would be no conscious subject for reflexive consciousness to objectify.

To put it in this way: Consciousness is the self-awareness that allows me to utter the "I" in "I see a house over there." In reflexive self-awareness the subject and its operation are objectified; and I then say, "I apprehend that I see a house over there." It is the difference between the conscious act of seeing a house, in which one is conscious of the house, and the reflexive consciousness, in which one is conscious of oneself seeing the house. Notice, however, that while the "I" of the first operation is now the object of the reflexive act, the "I" appears again as subject of the second operation, "I apprehend." When objectified, the "I" is not removed as subject, but, as it were, doubled. The basic subjective awareness intrinsic to conscious acts is an irreducible experience which, although it can be made the object of reflection and knowledge, cannot be replaced by any objective awareness, even of the self, nor adequately expressed in the language of objectivity.

The possibility of making the self the object of attention and knowledge creates a distinction between "I" and "me." "Me" is the self as made object. I am not, however, directly concerned here with the young child's use of "me" when it precedes the use of "I." "Me does this" or "Me wants that," says the child. This shows that consciousness itself is not yet fully developed; in particular, that the levels of intelligent and moral consciousness have not fully emerged. Further, reflexive self-awareness is as a consequence only rudimentary. The child does not clearly distinguish the way it is related to its own body and actions from its relationship with the bodies and actions of others and with the things around. Hence it refers to itself in a third-person fashion by using "me."

The child has not yet grasped its subjectivity sufficiently to use subjective language. A minimum self-image or reflexive grasp of the self would seem to be required for at least the fluent use of subjective terms and expressions.

The manner in which an adult uses "me," when all levels of conscious activity are in operation, is different. It does not then replace "I." Instead, it doubles it in reflection. The basic subjectivity of the "I" is objectified in a self-image as "me." It is true that this can be done in such a fashion that the person treats himself or part of himself as a mere object or thing, and is thus engaged in a process of self-alienation. But that need not be so. The path to genuine self-knowledge is also through objectification in reflection. Conscious acts, in their original self-awareness or basic subjectivity, become data that the subject considers and reflects upon, interprets and understands, explains and evaluates, knows and appropriates in a process of self-knowledge. Nor is that an enterprise of merely theoretical interest. Self-knowledge liberates, and reflexive self-awareness is a means of enlightenment and emancipation.

We may, then, make a distinction between self-being and self-knowledge. By self-being I mean the degree and manner in which the potential self has been actualized as shown in the range and quality of its conscious activity. At any given moment a person in his growth and development has reached a particular level of actual being as a self. That is his self-being. Self-knowledge is the extent to which the self knows its own reality in reflexive consciousness. Self-being and self-knowledge are interdependent. Without a good measure of self-knowledge a person will be greatly hindered in his development. More importantly, self-knowledge is an element in self-being; reflexive self-consciousness constitutes a high level of conscious activity. On the contrary, defects in self-being will block self-knowledge. Nevertheless, the two are not identical. Thus, a person's self-being and actions may be at a higher level than his self-knowledge. It seems useful, therefore, to take each by itself in turn.

Men do not come into existence ready-made. They have their being only through a long period of growth. Moreover, as historical beings men are subject to continuous change; their self-being is in a constant process of development or decline. Ideally, the growth and development of each person should be the unfolding of the intrinsic dynamism of his being in freedom, in creative interaction with the world, and in unconstrained communication with others.

Man's being as potential has, I maintain, a finality or dynamic thrust toward his fulfillment as a self. Man is not clay, passive under moulding in any and every way by external forces, whether natural or social. True, the openness of man's being as spiritual to all reality allows an infinite variety of modes in which his being can be actualized in relation with reality. However, the finality of man's being makes a demand for freedom, creativity, and communication, which condemns many situations and modes of life as inhuman because blocking a genuinely human fulfillment. The unfolding of man's being is a realization of his freedom. Human freedom is not a faculty or act alongside others; it is an attribute of man's conscious being as a whole. It is an original and inalienable characteristic of man, and may be best understood as man's possession of his own being. Man belongs to himself in a fundamental way as subject. Man is never simply nature, a thing, but always a person, always in relation to himself. His self-being is a self-possession manifested in the self-presence of consciousness. (I am leaving aside for the moment the question whether such freedom can be understood or preserved outside of a constitutive relationship to transcendent being.)[5]

The deployment of freedom in the concrete implies that any genuine development of self-being will be marked by an essential autonomy. Man must make himself; he must himself actualize his own potentiality as a self; he cannot be made as a person by others. The transition to full personhood from the immaturity of childhood is when the person recognizes that he must take charge of his own life and that he is responsible for what he becomes. Man as free is a self-constituting subject. And in a sense freedom is inescapable, because the very refusal of responsibility for our own becoming, to drift instead in conformity to external pressures, is an exercise of freedom. We use freedom to deny freedom.

Man's becoming is a becoming in a world. It takes place in a creative interaction with the persons, institutions, and things that make up the world, both natural and social, in which a man comes to be.

The natural and the social are inextricably intertwined. Nature now meets men only as transformed by the work of generations; in other words, it is mediated socially and historically. At the same time, nature remains underlying society, and the form of society depends upon the particular relationship with nature achieved through technology. Nature and society, then, in a particular combination, constitute the world in active, responsive relation with which each man attains his self-being.

So, while there is an intrinsic dynamism or potentiality in each man, it is actualized only as a response to reality as encountered. The degree and mode of its actualization, therefore, depends upon the natural and social context. Again, although every man is essentially free as a self, so that once personhood has emerged in the adult, the individual has a self-possession and self-presence marking him off as an autonomous being from the rest of nature, the range of effective freedom; that is, the extent and manner in which freedom can be exercised in the concrete is measured by social and natural conditions. Thus there is a history of human freedom, an unfolding of freedom through many generations on a scale greater than the life of the individual.

We can express the creative interaction between the self and the world in terms of the subject-object relationship. The subject-object relationship emerges from a preceding totality. That totality remains as the context in which the relationship is set. Subject and object are not, therefore, two entirely heterogeneous realities linked together in an external fashion. There is a bond of mutual participation between them that precedes their distinction and remains underlying it. The self emerges within the world and remains part of it. Its development depends upon the richness of its responsive relationship to the realities that constitute the world. If it isolates itself from the world and becomes alienated from it, so that subject and object are regarded as at two opposite poles in a tension without mutual participation, the subject or self becomes a thin, starved simulacrum of what it should be.

The world as social is a network of related selves. We thus pass to the third requirement for the growth and development of the self, namely, communication with others.

Only in and through relations with other selves does the individual self emerge, grow, and become autonomous. Only in and through relations with other selves can that autonomy be exercised fruitfully and move the person to fulfillment. Distortions in communication among selves is at once reflected in distortions in self-being. Ideally, communication should be unconstrained. By that I mean it should be free from domination or attempts at domination and be nonmanipulative in not treating other selves as things but fully respecting their freedom and creative autonomy.

The ideal of an unfolding of the self in freedom, creative interaction and unconstrained communication has not in fact been realized. Hence it is necessary to look at the obstacles that beset the self in its development and result in a defective self-being.

Like all that grows, the self is subject to accidents that cause blocks, quirks, and twists in subsequent development. Accidents in this instance may in general terms be said to be due to a disproportion between the self at a given moment of its development and the reality impinging upon it. As a consequence of the disproportion, the self is unable to respond adequately and resorts to some subterfuge or expedient, and this brings about a block, a division of the self, a repression. I have already mentioned, for example, that according to Janov's primal therapy, neurosis is caused by feelings being suppressed because their pain was intolerable. Internal barriers are then built up within the self as so many shields to protect the self against the feelings it continues to deny. Other psychologists give different accounts of the formation of neuroses and structures of repression. But all would agree in the general statement that the self, because unable to meet a challenge, dodges it in some manner that distorts the future course of its development.

Most problems of self-development involve other people and are created at least in part by a defect in communication. From the beginning the self has to struggle for emergence in its own autonomy in relation with parents and significant others. Even when of outstanding good will, parents and others bear the defects of their own past and of their present situation. After the vicissitudes of the parent-child relationship, the child, now adult, enters into a set of social relationships which for the most part rest upon structures of domination rather than of freedom. He is also lured into a labyrinth of manipulative communication. The result is predictable. Prior to the attainment of an adequate self-awareness, the individual has imposed upon him and internalizes attitudes and responses, modes of behavior, and forms of relationship that do not express his own freedom and creativity and are in fact incompatible with them.

The resultant self wears as many different costumes as an actor. Falsity is manifold; only truth is one. We all play many roles and put on many masks. Which is our authentic self? Divided internally as we are by barriers set up to shut off our true feelings and thoughts, because they were too painful or because they clashed with social conventions or the expectations of others, we do not know which is our true self. So much so that some have supposed that no matter how many masks we strip off, there is always another mask beneath. The self would then be entirely a social construct, a set of roles created and imposed upon us by society.

Usually, indeed, the human face is a succession of masks. We see the various social masks: the mask of the professor, the doctor, the policeman, the parent, the executive. However, if we observe long and carefully enough, moments of relaxation occur, the face is momentarily uncontrolled, the social mask drops, and we glimpse the real self beneath, in its pain and longing, in its serenity or fear, in its lovingness or bitterness, in its clarity or bewilderment.

The true self is hidden from ourselves as well as from others. Part of our growth in self-being is the effort to know the self. Besides the "I" of self-being, there is the "me" of self-knowledge. Clearly, it is easiest to know the plurality of our social selves. Hence "me" evokes in the first place the professorial me, the parental me, the executive me, and so forth. But the true me is what I am most fundamentally to myself when in a quiet moment I face what I know I am. But then the question still remains: Does that me correspond to what I am in reality?

Like all knowledge, self-knowledge is subject to the limitations of the knower. Something cannot become an object of knowledge unless it lies within the range or horizon of the knowing subject. At a particular stage of development the subject may not be able even to raise questions about a particular class of objects because they

are right beyond the horizon of his experience and thinking. In the case of self-knowledge, it can therefore hap-
pen, and often does, that the reality of the self is outside
the range of the self's knowing. The self is thus incapable
of knowing its own reality, unless it undergoes a transformation that expands its consciousness. Because of
that, self-knowledge is not a smooth process of advancing
insight, but an affair of leaps and upheavals, of
conversion-type experiences, brought about by a happy
combination of circumstances or, more importantly, by
the help of perceptive counselors and communities of
support.

Another great obstacle to self-knowledge is the resistance it meets with from the self, preventing the transformation of consciousness required. The reason for the
resistance is the threat self-knowledge offers to the present reality of the self. In the absence of genuine self-
knowledge, the self, for purposes of living, has formed a
self-image and created a structure, even if unstable,
among the various elements of the divided self. An in-
rush of self-knowledge would cause the collapse of that
structure, and the self fears, though wrongly, for its
identity and reality. Hence, it resists, tenaciously and with
great ingenuity, every advance in self-knowledge.

There is also a deeper fear, a fear, the mystics tell us,
experienced in the course of the mystical ascent. This is
the fear of the loss of the self as present in ordinary
consciousness, the empirical ego of everyday experience,
when we withdraw into the inmost or interior self and
become one with the transcendent. We are afraid to
confront the deepest reality of the self that we are, because that deepest self is beyond our individual reality
and consciousness and reveals their transitoriness and
finitude.

I come back to the problem with which I started this
chapter. True though my account of the growth and
development of the self may be, it deals, so it might be

argued, with what is comparatively unimportant because it would seem to concern only the empirical self. There has been an hypertrophy of individual consciousness in the West, the argument might continue, which has led to the isolated ego of modern alienated man and, in the context of Western theism, to the death of God or loss of transcendence. What is needed, the argument might conclude, is not a revamping of the Western concern with the individual self in its autonomy and development, but a return to the teaching that the deepest center of the self is beyond the individual ego.

What, then, has been the history of the self in the West? The starting point was the distinctively Christian emphasis upon the individual. The Christian emphasis differed from the Greek and Hellenistic idea of the freedom of the individual. That began as the freedom of the citizen within the community of the city-state and embraced the qualities of character fitting for the free citizen. It developed as an inner freedom or independence from everything that met man from without, including his own body. Such inner independence was given by the life of reason. Being an individual, being one's self, being free: all meant to possess one's self in rational thought.

Christian individualism was grounded instead upon a new sense of history and the accompanying conviction of the importance of the historical existence of each man. The new sense of history in Christianity derives from the eschatological worldview it took over from Jewish apocalyptic. Briefly, eschatology, which is about the *eschata* or last things, saw history as leading to a definite goal in accordance with God's plan. In that context the coming of Christ was seen as the decisive, once-for-all action of God, moving history to its end. Many difficult questions arise here: the interpretation of the apocalyptic imagery of the course of world history and its end; the Christian modification of the eschatological hope; the problematic character of any philosophy of history that attempts to interpret history as a whole. Only one basic point is relevant to our present purpose; namely, that history was regarded as meaningful in its own right, in a manner distinct from nature or the cosmos, with the consequence that attention in considering history was drawn to the future, not just to the past.

Rudolf Bultmann writes:

> To the Greeks, history does not come into consideration as an independent world alongside the world of the cosmos conceived of as nature. Naturally the varied course of the concrete historical event, and the differentiation of historical phenomena (seen in the first instance as one with the geographical phenomena), doubtless early aroused the interest of the Greeks. . . . But it remained hidden that history places man and the human community in a special sphere of living of their own, making the present a time for decision, in which responsibility towards the future and so also for the past is to be seized.[6]

The new sense of history altered the conception of human existence. Man no longer found the purpose of his existence in realizing the idea of man, in being an instance of a universal form, Man, to which the individual was subsidiary. Man now finds his real being in his concrete, historical life. To quote Bultmann again:

> His being is fulfilled not in the universal, but in the individual. His past is *his* past, which inescapably stamps him with its blessing or its curse. His future is *his* future, not standing before him as the image of an ideal to which he more and more conforms in an upward struggle, but a future which is to be chosen in responsible decision with the risk of attaining to himself or losing himself.[7]

"This individualism," remarks Bultmann a little later, "then released a force of reflection (as it is primarily a religious phenomenon)—that is, the consciousness that one is standing alone in the presence of God and must give account of oneself before him."[8]

With those words we meet the self of Christian interiority, the interior self defined by its relationship to God, prominent in Augustine and subsequently in Western Christendom. But before we turn to Augustine, a further point must be made about the biblical account of man.

As an historical being, standing as an individual in the presence of God, each man was seen as placed over against the world, no longer a cosmic being. That transcendence of the world or, in other words, the nonworldly nature of the self, was intensified by gnostic influences. Christianity never accepted the gnostic view that the world was not the creation of God but of a lower, evil power, but it did hold an historical form of dualism, according to which in this evil age the world is given over to Satan, who is "the god of this world" (2 Cor. 4:4). Christians, therefore, are foreigners in the world: "For here we have no lasting city, but we seek the city which is to come" (Heb. 13:14); and "our commonwealth is in heaven" (Phil. 3:20).

In a somewhat paradoxical fashion, therefore, the Christian sense of history led to a conception of the self as a transcendent entity, standing alone as an individual before God and placed over against the world, different from everything belonging to the world. In brief, the self was conceived as an interior self or nonworldly being, in but not of the world. And this conception was linked to a negative evaluation of the world in this present age.

Augustine is the exemplary instance at the beginning of Western culture of the experience of the interior self as standing alone in the presence of God. His *Confessions* are an expression of that experience. To "confess" is to give an account of oneself before God. In writing what is the first autobiography. Augustine presents a dialogue of the self with God. He wrote indeed with readers in mind, but the whole book is addressed to God and is penetrated with the sense that God is the chief listener.

The self for Augustine is a "transphenomenal abyss."[9] He writes in his commentary on Psalm XLI:

> If by "abyss" we understand a great depth, is not man's heart, do you not suppose, *an abyss*? For what is there more profound than that "abyss"? Men may speak, may be seen by the operations of their members, may be heard speaking in conversation: but whose thought be penetrated, whose heart seen into? What he is inwardly engaged on, what he is inwardly capable of, what he is inwardly doing or what purposing, what he is inwardly wishing to happen, or not to happen, who shall comprehend? . . . Do not you believe that there is in man a "deep" so profound as to be hidden even to him in whom it is?[10]

It is in the depths of that interior self we meet the transcendent light of God. As we read in the *Confessions:*

> Being admonished by all this to return to myself, I entered into my own depths with You as guide; and I was able to do it because You were my helper. I entered, and with the eye of my soul, such as it was, I saw Your unchangeable Light shining over that same eye of my soul, over my mind. It was not the light of everyday that the eye of flesh can see, nor some greater light of the same order, such as might be if the brightness of our daily light should be seen shining with a more intense brightness and filling all things with its greatness. Your Light was not that, but other, altogether other, than all such lights.[11]

For Augustine, as Thomas Prufer says: "The self is constituted in listening and speaking to God; it is no longer primarily constituted as a being in the world."[12]

But this self, nonworldly in nature, not merely transcends the world, but is alienated from it:

> Every man in this life is a foreigner: in which life ye see that with flesh we are covered round, through which flesh the heart cannot be seen . . . in this sojourning of fleshly life every one carrieth his own heart, and every heart to every other heart is shut.[13]

There is, then, a cleavage between the interior self, constituted by its relationship with God, and the self as it appears in this world and is seen in the flesh by others. Augustine thus anticipated modern subjectivism with his conception of a noumenal self set over against a phenomenal world, including the body and the lower psyche. Indeed, when in the *De Trinitate* he treats of the mind's knowledge of itself, he gives the same account of self-certitude as Descartes did centuries later. He says:

> But since we treat of the nature of the mind, let us remove from our consideration all knowledge which is received from without, through the senses of the body; and attend more carefully to the position which we have laid down, that all minds know and are certain concerning themselves. . . . Yet who ever doubts that he himself lives, and remembers, and understands, and wills, and thinks, and knows, and judges? Seeing that even if he doubts, he lives; if he doubts, he remembers why he doubts; if he doubts, he understands that he doubts; if he doubts, he wishes to be certain; if he doubts, he thinks; if he doubts, he knows that he does not know; if he doubts, he judges that he ought not to assent rashly. Whosoever therefore doubts about anything else, ought not to doubt of all these things; which if they were not, he would not be able to doubt of anything.[14]

Nevertheless, the transition from the interiority of Augustine to the subjectivism of Descartes marks a great change in Western consciousness. The change involved may be briefly stated by saying that modern subjectivism represents a secularization of Christian interiority. In other words, the nonworldly self was retained after the constitutive relationship with God was ignored or rejected. The isolation of the self from God as well as from the world led to idealism, the death of God, nihilism, and that diffuse sense of loneliness and loss vaguely referred to as modern alienation.

At the beginning of modern subjectivism, Descartes established a dichotomy between the self, constituted by thought, and the body, constituted by extension and understood in purely mechanical terms with the rest of the material universe. Moreover, although Descartes himself affirmed God, his system is essentially atheistic, because the dogmatic rationalism of his philosophy and his mechanistic account of the universe left only an accidental role for God. Further, for Descartes, the mind, isolated in its doubting from God and the world, regained God and indirectly the world simply by its own cognitive power. Hence, despite his affirmations, the nonworldly self, the subject isolated from the world, is now in effect launched on a course without God.

The subject, experiencing itself outside the world, over against it as its object, was tempted to constitute its own world out of itself, perhaps remembering its previous oneness with the world-constituting intellect and will of God.[15] It succumbed to that temptation in German idealism and more diffusely in the widespread modern tendency to find the foundation and criterion of all reality in the subject. The isolated ego, spinning the world out of itself, resulted in the death of God and in nihilism.

The consequence of the dichotomy of subject and object, and the fading of the conviction that the self or subject was constituted by its relationship with God as its deepest center, was the inability to experience God as immanent. God became only an object, over against the subject, an object among other objects. The loss of immanence destroyed true transcendence. Only its semblance remained in the placing of God as object at an infinite distance from the subject. This made God so remote that he eventually disappeared over the horizon of infinite space. The Victorians thus struggled with the disappearance of God, with the absence or hiddenness of God. But as J. Hillis Miller observes in a brilliant essay: "A God who has disappeared from nature and from the human heart can come to be seen not as invisible but as nonexistent. The unseen God of Arnold or Tennyson becomes the dead God of Nietzsche. If the disappearance of God is presupposed by much Victorian poetry, the death of God is the starting point for many twentieth-century writers."[16]

"Man has killed God by separating his subjectivity from everything but itself."[17] The death of God is the consequence of the transition from the interior self to the isolated ego, which has taken place in Western culture. The interior self was nonworldly, but it defined itself in relation to God, the Creator of the world. The isolated ego defines everything outside itself in relation to itself, viewing it merely as the object of its intellect and will. The further consequence is nihilism. J. Hillis Miller writes:

> When God and the creation become objects of consciousness, man becomes a nihilist. Nihilism is the nothingness of consciousness when consciousness becomes the foundation of everything. Man the murderer of God and drinker of the sea of creation wanders through the infinite nothingness of his own ego. Nothing now has any worth except the arbitrary value he sets on things as he assimilates them into his consciousness.[18]

What is the way out of modern nihilism? It is not, I want to argue, through a further withdrawal into the self in an attempt to find God again by an increased spiritualization. The remedy lies rather in the expansion of consciousness outward into the world to rediscover God as immanent in reality.

The "interior self" is a misleading phrase. What is conceived in terms of depth as the interior self might be more aptly thought of as the centered self in contrast to the self as scattered or fragmented or, perhaps, to the distracted self. In any event, the human self at its deepest level or center is not a disembodied self. Man's true subjectivity is not the self-sufficient independence of an isolated monad, but a self-possessed openness to the plenitude of being. As an embodied subjectivity, the self participates in that plenitude of being only in and through the world with which it is bodily one. Only as one with the world does it meet God as immanent both in the world and in itself as the consciousness of the world.

True interiority is, therefore, correlative with sensuousness; that is, with the open responsiveness of the embodied person to reality. A canker in Christian interiority from the beginning, infected as it was by gnosticism, was a negative attitude to the world. The self that turns away from the world does not however find self-transcendence, but is driven instead to a shrill self-sufficiency. Participation in the world is replaced by manipulation of the world, sensuousness by sensuality. Precisely because it stresses the individual in a way the Eastern traditions do not, Christianity, to remain healthy, has to take special care not to sever the self from its participation in the world. Individualism without participation produces that caricature of the Christian individual which is the isolated ego—aggressive, manipulative, and possessive because of its own emptiness.

In his book, *The Poetry of Reality,* from which I have already quoted, J. Hillis Miller examines the related ways in which a group of modern writers—Yeats, Eliot, Dylan Thomas, Wallace Stevens, and William Carlos Williams—have found a way out of the experience of nihilism into a new sense of reality. In his introductory essay he outlines the common features of their escape from subjectivism and nihilism. The act that has led to nihilism is that by which man has turned the world into his own mind; man must now reverse the process and turn himself into the world. He must, in Wallace Steven's phrase, "step barefoot into reality."[19]

This implies, first, the effacement of the ego before reality. Men must abandon the will to power over things. "When man is willing to let things be then they appear in a space which is no longer that of an objective world opposed to the mind. In this new space the mind is dispersed everywhere in things and forms one with them."[20] Secondly, the dimension of depth is also given up. Objects are no longer separated from the mind and detached from one another in a predominantly visual space, with God at an infinite distance beyond. "The space of separation is turned inside-out, so that elements once dispersed are gathered together in a new region of copresence. . . . The mind, its objects, other minds, and the ground of both mind and things are present in a single realm of proximity."[21] Thirdly, "If any spiritual power can exist for the new poetry it must be an immanent presence. . . . If there is to be a God in the new world it must be a presence within things and not beyond them."[22]

I cannot resist quoting at least one expression of the new immediacy, which brings together subject and object, imagination and reality, in a copresence of being, including the spiritual. I choose this section of Wallace Stevens's poem, "An Ordinary Evening in New Haven"*:

> We keep coming back and coming back
> To the real: to the hotel instead of the hymns
> That fall upon it out of the wind. We seek
>
> The poem of pure reality, untouched
> By trope or deviation, straight to the word,
> Straight to the transfixing object, to the object
>
> At the exactest point at which it is itself,
> Transfixing by being purely what it is,
> A view of New Haven, say, through the certain eye,
>
> The eye made clear of uncertainty, with the sight
> Of simply seeing, without reflection. We seek
> Nothing beyond reality. Within it,
>
> Everything, the spirit's alchemicana
> Included, the spirit that goes roundabout
> And through included, not merely the visible,
>
> The solid, but the movable, the moment,
> The coming on of feasts and the habits of saints,
> The pattern of the heavens and high, night air.[23]

The approach to reality found by J. Hillis Miller in modern poetry is paralleled by the attitude advocated independently by the artist Frederick Franck in *The Zen of Seeing*. He distinguishes between "looking" and "seeing":

> The purpose of "looking" is to survive, to cope, to manipulate, to discern what is useful, agreeable, or threatening to the Me, what enhances or what diminishes the Me. This we are trained to do from our first day. When, on the other hand, I SEE—suddenly I am all eyes, I forget this Me, am liberated from it and dive into the reality of what confronts me, become part of it, participate in it.[24]

The eye with which we thus see "is the eye not of the Me, but of 'God born in man's soul,' of the true Self."[25]

I am admitting, then, that there has indeed been an hypertrophy of individual consciousness in the West. The true self has been lost sight of and the scene dominated instead by the isolated subject, nihilistic in its endeavors to find the foundation of all reality in its own consciousness, and manipulative in its treatment of the rest of reality as mere objects of its thought, will, and action. I am also arguing that the return from the isolated ego to the true self is through a new relationship with reality, a relationship of participation in which the subject experiences the mutual immanence between itself and objects, between itself and other subjects, between itself and the transcendent ground of all subjects and objects. By participation it enters into a copresence with the objects and subjects to which it responds, and is led by the dynamic of its response to the mysterious plenitude of being, of which all subjects and objects, including itself, are finite manifestations.

In human living the relation of participation is what I have described as sensuousness in contrast to sensuality, which is the concrete form of the nonparticipatory, instrumental relationship to the world. I am urging, in effect, a change from the pornographic sensibility that has developed in the West—for which the world is a prostitute to be mounted with lust or rejected with loathing—to an erotic sensibility, for which the world is to be affectionately caressed and embraced with a self-forgetting love.

But the question is whether the Christian emphasis on the individual, based as it is upon a new sense of history, can be joined to an erotic sensibility and the participatory attitude to the world this implies.

The new sense of history severed man from the cosmos as no longer a cosmic being. Would it not have been a more adequate conception to say instead that the cosmos ceases to be cosmos, because it has been taken up into human history and, no longer an unchangeable order, shares the openness of mankind to the future? The natural sciences deal in universal laws because they are abstract; any consideration of nature in the concrete reality of its individual entities and events would have to be historical and linked to human history. Nature and history are inseparably interwoven in their actuality. So, instead of its placing man over against nature, the new sense of history could be seen as closely binding nature to man.

I have already discussed in the previous chapter what I consider the misinterpretation of the present disorder of the human condition, and I have argued that the impossibility of a first innocence for men is not rooted in rebellious bodily impulses, nor is second innocence achieved by rational control. The disorder arises from man's abuse of his higher potentialities and is encountered by the self-transcending affectivity of sensuousness. The attempt to meet the disorder by a rationally controlled withdrawal from the world creates a pornographic sensibility and an asceticism which is but the reverse side of sensuality.

Nevertheless, the attitude to the world cannot be unqualifiedly positive. Because of the intertwining of nature and history, we experience nature and the body only as penetrated and moulded by human intentions, meanings, and purposes, not all of which are good. Add to this the fact that human society in considerable measure consists of socially fixated sin and the derivative disorders. The result is that the world, both natural and social, as we experience it in the concrete has often to be struggled against and resisted as an enemy, so that we become like foreigners in a strange land. The sayings of the New Testament and of Christian writers like Augustine are true if taken phenomenologically and dialectically; namely, as expressing one side of the actual, concrete experience which men have of the world. But they have been interpreted undialectically as if they were the total expression of man's relationship with the world. The undialectical interpretation has given them an ontological force as expressing the essential relationship of man and the world, so that, despite the theoretical rejection of the gnostic account of the world as evil, in practice the gnostic attitude has infected Christian praxis.

Is, then, the interior self nonworldly or not? I should agree that the deepest self of man is constituted by its relationship with the transcendent God. Man has a capacity for the infinite, and the actualization of that capacity in a response to the transcendent constitutes the deepest level of his self-being. Moreover, the self at that level cannot be simply identified with the self as it appears in everyday experience nor with the many social roles or selves. But all the other levels of man's self-being and all his worldly relationships are to be seen as mediating the deepest actuality of the self. If the Christian symbol of the resurrection means anything, it means that God's relationship with the human self is not with an isolated ego, but with a self in the world, and that the self-being and self-destiny of men are part, even if the highest and determinative part, of the total being and total destiny of the world.

But is not the interior self beyond any individual self and simply one with transcendent reality? Therefore, in

Christian terms, is it not on the side of God the transcendent, not on the side of the world from whom God is and remains distinct? However, even if we allow that the blurring of the distinction between the self of religious experience and the ego of superficial experience and rational consciousness is a distortion of Christian individualism, we must still affirm that, despite the language of some of its mystics, the mainstream of the Christian tradition refuses to identify the inmost self with God and insists upon an individual destiny for the individual.

The Christian insistence upon the individual self may best be seen in the context of the doctrine of the Trinity. It then becomes apparent that what is important is relationship rather than distinction as such. The teaching of three persons in one God implies that not merely absolute qualities—power, truth, goodness, and so on—but also relationships are found at the level of ultimate reality. The persons in the Trinity are distinct, not by any absolute quality, but solely by their relationships. Relationships, therefore, are seen as constitutive of transcendent reality. In contrast, the implications of any monistic world-view is that relationships are not ultimately real. They are then merely aspects of transitoriness and finitude, fugitive combinations of appearances, left behind as we become one with the really real.

We are confronted here with two different total accounts of reality. The question of the identity or distinction of the interior self and ultimate reality cannot be taken as a thesis on its own. The debate should be between two world views, one for which relationships are of ultimate significance and one for which they are not. The key relationships in this regard are personal relationships. The criterion will be the comparative adequacy of each view to human experience.

A further reason for referring to the doctrine of the Trinity in this context is that Trinitarianism, more clearly than simple theism, refuses to see God as an object over against the subject. Part of the meaning of the doctrine is the immanence of God in both subject and object. The subject-object distinction is thus transcended, though not removed.

There is a close relationship between the doctrine of the Trinity and that of creation. The Father is God as the transcendent creator, the Logos or Son is the Word of God expressed and immanent in creation as objectified meaning, and the Spirit is the responsive love of God expressed and immanent in conscious subjects. Just as the Word and the Spirit are one, yet distinct, so also subject and object are one, yet distinct. Just as Word and Spirit are together one with the Father, yet distinct from him, so also the self-in-the-world is one with the transcendent creator, yet distinct from him. The relationships at the level of creation are a participation in the relationships of the Trinity itself. The eternity of the relationships and of the distinctions they bring in the Trinity itself is reflected in the irrevocability of relationships and distinctions at the level of creation.

In brief, it is because God is a Trinity that his self-manifestation in creation is not in the form of a cosmos, but in the form of a history. History is an affair of what is concrete, particular, individual. We are present to God, not indeed as isolated egos, but as individual selves. The eternal significance we receive from our constitutive relationship with God belongs to us as particular, concrete, historical individuals.

IV.
Death and the Self

The new sense of history introduced by Christianity and the new evaluation of the individual it brought with it altered the experience and understanding of death.

Just as a man's life was no longer considered merely as an instance of human life in general, but as an individual life of particular, unique significance, so also a man's death was not now conceived as simply an instance of a universal, natural process, but as an event proper to the individual as *his* death, the conclusion to the unique life story that distinguished him as an individual. Moreover, because the individual was understood as constituted as a self by his relationship with God, death was seen as a moment of isolation in which the self stood alone in the presence of God.[1] Death became a truly awesome individual event, in which the self, stripped of all its transitory roles and relationships, all its repressions and self-deceptions, was naked and alone in its inmost reality before the transcendent God.

With a heightened individual self-awareness, the
event of death thus becomes fraught with anxiety, owing
both to its negative aspect of self-stripping or loss of all
the obvious supports of identity and to its positive aspect
of being the uncovering before God of the actual reality
and value of the self. In contrast, for example, death in
the early period of the Old Testament was seen as simply
a completely natural and normal process, unaccom-
panied by any anxiety, a peaceful ending to a fruitful life.
"Abraham breathed his last and died in a good old age,
an old man and full of years, and was gathered to his
people" (Gen. 25:8). "And Isaac breathed his last; and he
died and was gathered to his people, old and full of days;
and his sons Esau and Jacob buried him" (Gen. 35:29).
"When Jacob finished charging his sons, he drew up his
feet into the bed, and breathed his last, and was gathered
to his people" (Gen. 49:33). Death was, as Joshua described it, "the way of all the earth" (Joshua 23:14). There
was at that time no explicit thought of a future life. But
death was not seen as problematic or absurd; it was a
natural and unavoidable fact, a manifestation of the limited nature of human life. The individual with his own
destiny had not yet emerged from the people.[2]

Death, however, did become a problem as the Old
Testament period advanced. The expression of this was
the link established between death and sin. "Death," says
the Book of Wisdom, "was not God's doing, he takes no
pleasure in the extinction of the living" (1:13).[3] And the
Genesis story of creation presents death as a punishment
for the sin of our first parents, a feature of human existence brought into the world by man's sin.

The theme of sin and death was taken up by Paul
and elaborated by him in relation to Christ's death. Because of the centrality of Christ's death as a symbol, death
became intimately bound up with sin and redemption in
Christian consciousness. Paul's understanding of death is
apparent when we group together the following texts:

"Therefore as sin came into the world through one man and death through sin, and so death spread to all men because all men sinned" (Rom. 5:12). But "Christ died for our sins" (1 Cor. 15:3); he came "in the likeness of sinful flesh" (Rom. 8:3), but "he who has died is freed from sin" (Rom. 6:7). "The death he died he died to sin, once for all, but the life he lives he lives to God" (Rom. 6:10). So, "if we have been united with him in a death like his, we shall certainly be united with him in a resurrection like his" (Rom. 6:5). "We were buried therefore with him by baptism into death, so that as Christ was raised from the dead by the glory of the Father, we too might walk in newness of life" (Rom. 6:4). "Death is swallowed up in victory, O death, where is thy victory? O death, where is thy sting" (1 Cor. 15:54, 55). Nevertheless, "the last enemy to be destroyed is death" (1 Cor. 15:26), and so Christians still have to face death "always carrying in the body the death of Jesus, so that the life of Jesus may also be manifested in our bodies. For while we live we are always being given up to death for Jesus' sake" (2 Cor. 4:10, 11). Christians may, like Paul himself, come to long for physical death to complete their union with Christ: "My desire is to depart and be with Christ" (Phil. 1:23).

Paul, then, sees death in the context of a redemptive process of reversal, in which the consequences of sin are made the means of redemption. Death, the result of sin, now has a fourfold redemptive meaning for the Christian. First, we have all died in Christ. Death in this first sense means the share we all have in the death of Christ insofar as Christ by his death has altered the situation of mankind. Second, we are baptized into his death. Baptism is a death by which we die with Christ to sin. Third, there is a daily dying. We have to live out our baptism in our daily lives, dying to sin with Christ's death and living with his risen life. Fourth, physical death is the completion of our baptism and of our daily dying; our earthly bodies are destroyed, so that we can be at home with Christ.

Here, in short, is an understanding of death that makes it the expression and completion of human existence as a whole, whether that existence is one of sin in Adam or one of redeemed life in Christ. Before we grapple with the problems it raises, it might help to look at the way some other religious traditions handle death.[4]

The Buddhist tradition presupposes the wheel of existence as a cycle of rebirths and redeaths. For it, therefore, life in this world and death are brought together as equal features of the unsatisfactory human condition from which release is sought in nirvana. Buddhism admits a certain indestructibility of the individual, inasmuch as the individual goes on everlastingly from one rebirth and redeath to another rebirth and redeath, until nirvana is achieved. But, although there is thus an individual current of existence passing through successive lives, there is no permanent self. Liberation from the cycle is not the release of a self, and it leaves all individuality behind because nirvana is beyond the realm of change to which individual existence belongs.

There are also heavens and hells in the Buddhist world picture, and rebirth into one of these, according to merits and demerits, is a possibility. Nevertheless, these higher and lower regions are all part of the impermanent existence, essentially unsatisfactory, from which nirvana is the deliverance. In other words, not death, but life itself is the existential problem for Buddhism. Human life is essentially unsatisfactory. Everything is *dukkha*, namely, "ill-fare" or, as usually translated, "suffering." But the hope should not be for individual immortality in some paradise, because the individual, constituted by change, is marked by essential impermanence. Hope should be directed to the permanence of nirvana.

Death has indeed some prominence in Buddhist literature, not as a special problem, but as a striking sign of the impermanence of the world and human life. Hence, also the Buddhist practice of meditating upon death, sometimes gruesomely, as at the burning ground amid the charred remains of cremated corpses. Death, therefore, is not passed over by the Buddhist tradition as though it were merely a biological event of no religious significance. Nor is it rendered acceptable by being seen in religious hope as the prelude to a happy individual life in another world. Death is confronted and accepted as the chief sign of the impermanence of all human life, in order by this acceptance to achieve a transcendence of both life and death in a permanent state beyond all change and all individual existence.

A similar approach to death is found in Advaita Vedānta, the most influential school of the Hindu tradition. The difference lies in the Hindu recognition of a permanent self, the ātman, the true and eternal self, beyond the empirical self. Liberation thus becomes oneness of the ātman with Brahman, the ultimate reality or Absolute. This liberation, however, does not bring any essential change in state; it is simply the realization of that inner, eternal, unchangeable oneness of the true self with Brahman. The overcoming of death is the same as the overcoming of birth; namely, a release from the cycle of phenomenal existence through a shift in consciousness that brings a transcendence of the experience and categories of the empirical world.

Consequently, for this form of Hinduism, as for Buddhism, life, not death, is the problem, and the unsatisfactoriness of phenomenal existence is an essential feature of it, not an accidental disorder due to sin. Death is accepted as a sign of that unsatisfactoriness in an effort to transcend both life and death in the realization of a transphenomenal oneness with the one true reality.

Other schools in the Hindu tradition share that approach to death. The two closely linked schools of Samkhya and Yoga see ultimate reality as a plurality of eternal souls, so that liberation is not the entry into an essentially new, future form of existence, but the reconquest of what is always one's essential, true, transphenomenal reality.

However, a less austere attitude to death and liberation developed in both the Buddhist and the Hindu traditions. The original Buddhist attitude was modified in the "Pure Land" doctrine, which emerged in Mahāyāna Buddhism. The Pure Land of the great Buddha, Amitabha (in Japanese, Amida), was a place to which those who called upon his name went after death, where the conditions for attaining liberation were most favorable. Conceived as a paradise, it soon served to satisfy the desire for immediate salvation, and its splendors and availability tended to obscure the long and difficult quest for nirvana in the minds of the ordinary run of devotees. It gave Buddhism belief in a heavenly afterlife similar to the Christian belief.

The theistic schools of the Hindu tradition, such as those of Ramanuja and Madhva, likewise offered devotees a life of happiness in union with God in heaven. The Pure Land paradise of Mahāyāna Buddhism and the heaven of the theistic Hindu schools imply, it seems to me, a profoundly different attitude to death than that of original Buddhism and monistic Hinduism. In the latter case, death is confronted and accepted as a fearsome sign of the illusory, impermanent nature of empirical existence and its superficial categories, and as provoking a realization of what already and essentially is the true reality. In the former case, death becomes the prelude to a future, paradisal state, conceived imaginatively as the happiness and fulfillment of the individual person. Death closes one chapter of human existence but opens another, hopefully a better one.

The difference lies indeed in the place of hope in human existence. Of its nature, hope looks to the not-yet, to the future. We do not, properly speaking, hope for what already is or for what we already are or have. While, then, in primitive Buddhism and monistic Hinduism, there is room for confidence that liberation will be achieved if the appropriate discipline is followed, hope in the strict sense for nirvana or for oneness with the Absolute would seem to be out of place. These are in themselves unchanging realities, and there is no individual self who will enter into possession of them and thus whose possession of them can be an object of hope. Liberation does not lead to the essentially new, but uncovers what permanently is, leaving behind what has appearance but no true reality. In contrast, in the Pure Land school of Buddhism, in theistic Hinduism and, even more clearly, in Christianity with its belief in heaven, in personal immortality and in the resurrection, the category of the essentially new, the not-yet, becomes important. Hope in the proper sense is proclaimed in a new mode of existence, a new order of reality, to be enjoyed by these identical selves as individuals the other side of death.

But is such an otherworldly hope, a hope focused upon an afterlife, a life different from the one that we know, anything more than wishful thinking? Some would regard that form of hope as a neurotic escape from the misery or emptiness of the present into a dream of the future. That it is an escape is surely shown, it may be said, by its failure to face death for what it clearly is: the end of individual existence for embodied human persons. Death is denied in its function of manifesting the finitude of human existence, with harmful, destructive consequences for human living, both individual and social.

There are, I think, plausible grounds for arguing that Western culture has been afflicted with a neurosis of hope. The present has been emptied of stable meaning by various forms, first religious and then secular, of messianism, millenarianism, and utopianism, with the consequent restlessness endemic to Western man. Related to this has been the failure to face death, whether by smothering its reality in religious hope or, with the collapse of that hope, by the attempt to deny death, as in the grotesque pretences of the American customs satirized by Evelyn Waugh in *The Loved One* and in the British social denial and individual repudiation of mourning documented by Geoffrey Gorer in *Death, Grief and Mourning*.[5]

The denial of death is the denial of human finitude and the open sesame to every fantasy of the future. It has thus led to the excesses of a technological development uncontrolled by human values because of an unwillingness to admit any limitation. The conquest of death is now becoming more directly the aim of technology with advanced medical techniques, organic transplants, and biological engineering. Hopes are being expressed that death will indeed be conquered, so that in the future any death will be by accident or intent.[6] Meanwhile, the result of the refusal to admit death is the inability of many doctors and relatives to allow a person to die with human dignity as long as the bodily organism can still be lashed into vital motion by machines.

The denial of death, with its indulgence of our infantile wishes for omnipotence and immortality, does not remain harmless fantasy, but protects itself against reality by various forms of aggression. Elisabeth Kübler-Ross writes:

> If a whole nation, a whole society suffers from such a fear and denial of death, it has to use defenses which can only be destructive. Wars, riots, and increasing numbers of murders and other crimes may be indicators of our decreasing ability to face death with acceptance and dignity.[7]

It is not part of Kübler-Ross's purpose to question belief in an afterlife. Alan Watts, however, has connected hope for immortality and denial of death as the end of the individual person with a withdrawal from suffering and the consequent formation of an enclosed egocentric consciousness. He writes:

. . . we seek detachment from the body, wanting to convince ourselves that the real "I" is not this quaking mass of tissue with all its repulsive possibilities for pain and corruption. It is little wonder that we expect religions, philosophies, and other forms of wisdom to show us above all else a way of deliverance from suffering, from the plight of being a soft body in a world of hard reality. Sometimes therefore it seems that the answer is to match hardness with hardness, to identify ourselves with a spirit which has principles but no feelings, to despise and mortify the body, and to withdraw into the comfortably fleshless world of abstract thought or psychic fantasy.[8]

There is, then, a refusal of pain, a refusal to feel. We close off the self against feeling and pain. We thus create an unreal self and an unreal world based upon the exclusion of pain, suffering, and evil. But precisely because the world we make is unreal, it leads to a straining after the future. We escape into an unreal hope.

But the solution only aggravates the problem. First, the refusal to allow the organism its reaction to pain intensifies the suffering itself, and, secondly, the refusal of feeling contracts consciousness into a knot around its own center in an enclosed ego that is really a spasm of fear. And Alan Watts goes on to remark that "this shrinking of consciousness from our reactions to suffering is at root the same psychological mechanism as the straining of consciousness to get the most from our reactions to pleasure, and both make up the sensation of the separate, indwelling ego."[9]

A contracted consciousness is egocentric and, because it cuts the ego off from reality, it is also unreal. The emptiness of the unreal ego leads to sensuality or to compensatory fantasies of an ideal reality in the future—or perhaps to both. The opposite way of living is to relax into present reality and meet pain by an extension, not by a contraction, of consciousness. According to Watts, to expand consciousness is to feel an identity with the whole world, to realize that the ego is not the real "I," but that real "I" is nothing less than all that there is.[10]

This implies that death is "when our conventional identity comes to the end of its tether and we 'give up the ghost' of the isolated ego."[11] Watts challenges those who believe in the survival of the individual personality to think through what they mean. Do we really wish our limited individualities to go on indefinitely?—". . . the indefinite prolongation of the individual is bad design—architecturally, biologically, and psychologically."[12]

To face death for what it is as the end of individual existence enables one, so Watts contends, to find one's true identity as one with universal reality. To confront death as the end may also enable us to live without reserve, not just provisionally, in the present. A short scenario, written by William Hamilton, about the first day in the life of a college student after she has learned that she will shortly die of a fatal illness makes that point vividly. The girl, who is still unable to believe in immortality, says to her boyfriend:

> I seem to have come out from under a cloud of pressure that my life was determined by. . . . All the virtues I was taught to value—achievement, competence, social responsibility—were based on a future time when there would be less tension, less pressure. I was always getting ready, just about to do or be something, in training. But never really doing. Never really getting hold of "now," today, the present. . . . I feel for the first time in my life that I am free to live in the present moment without some censor peering over my shoulder with advice about postponing gratification or delight. Does it make sense to say that one only learns to live when one is about to die?[13]

We have, it seems, built up an unhealthy syndrome, of which hope for the continuance of the individual self beyond death is one of the elements: the refusal of pain and a withdrawal from feeling into a contracted consciousness, closed in upon the individual self; the distortion of sensuousness into sensuality, of participation in

the world into exploitation of it, with an inability to identify the inmost self with universal reality; the struggle to
compensate for the emptiness of the present with fantasies and dreams of the future; the refusal to accept
death and the attempt to denature it by turning it into a
prelude to paradise.

Should we therefore, with Alan Watts, reject the
Christian belief in the survival of the individual beyond
death and turn instead to some form of the Eastern
religious tradition, which in general sees death as the
return to the inmost self beyond the individual ego? I
myself am not willing to surrender the Christian emphasis upon the individual so quickly. But that unwillingness demands a closer look at the Christian conception of death.

The Bible, as we have seen, establishes a link between death and sin. Widely today among Christian
thinkers, the biblical story of creation and original sin is
no longer interpreted as history, but as a mythical narra-
tive symbolic of man's permanent condition. Likewise we
may leave aside the interpretation of sin and death that
takes the connection as causal, as though sin somehow
introduced and caused death. We are dealing with a
mythic expression of what death has become in the present state of human disorder. Death from that standpoint
is for Christians the visible, tangible appearance of sin.
Death is, as it were, sin itself in its corporeal, visible form.
Is that view of death an unhealthy repudiation of it? Is it
the surrounding of a natural event with guilt because of
infantile dreams of power and immortality? I do not
think so. It is a deep insight into the present human
condition.

What is sin? In Augustine's phrase, it is "self-love in
contempt of God."[14] It is precisely the turning of the self
back upon itself, so that it closes itself from reality and
makes itself the center of its own universe. It is the isolated, egocentric consciousness. It is the refusal of self-

transcendence. Man uses his freedom, his self-possessing and self-constituting subjectivity, to close himself upon himself, instead of opening himself to the plenitude of being. Death is the symbol of sin, because death, when taken solely in relation to man, is isolation.

Death is the severance of all human relationships; communication is broken off. The process of dying is a process of increasing isolation. And since, for the Christian, relationship with God is in and through relationship with others, in and through human community, death seems to cut the person off from God. "My God, my God, why hast thou forsaken me?" was the cry of Christ on the cross. And Augustine comments: it was "so as to signify the death of our soul, that those words were uttered, not only in the Psalm, but also on the cross."[15]

Sin is not just an individual but a social reality; it affects the way we live in society. A striking sign, then, of the sinful egocentric character of our present culture, with its multitude of enclosed selves pursuing their self-ish aims in isolation, is the fact that today most people die alone. Most people die in a hospital, usually with no one present. Relatives do not make vigil, and it is a matter of chance if a nurse or doctor happens to be present at the moment of death.

The transformation of death for the Christian from a symbol of sin into a symbol of new life in Christ was therefore appropriately expressed by the ritual that accompanied dying, wherever possible. The dying person was not left alone, but was reassured by the presence and prayers of relatives, neighbors, and priest of the continuance of his relationship with them and with God in Christ. To stay with the dying, to assure them of love with a touch of the hand, a look, a sensitivity to their unspoken needs, a praying with and for them without falsity, demands the ability to feel, the achievement of a spontaneity of response to the real situation, the attainment of a self-transcending sensuousness. The person must be able to feel the suffering and pain of others and to allow his own feelings of loss, grief, despair to arise. Someone who is egocentric, whose attitude to the world and others is manipulative and characterized by sensuality, will avoid being with the dying. Death represents a threat to his enclosed personality. Besides, he has refused that openness of response which is feeling, and there is now no other way of relating to the dying person, unless as a medical person he can limit his relationship to the purely technical.

Christian hope, therefore, in its authentic form does not imply any repudiation or avoidance of death, because it is in and through death that life is expected. While the link between death and sin has led at times to exaggerated depictions of the grimness and horror of death, it expresses the experience of death as isolation and has its counterpart in the Christian transformation of death by the loving presence of the community around the dying person. The widespread concern today with the needs of the dying should surely lead to the recognition that it is inhuman to leave a person to die alone without the loving presence of another human being.

The Christian tradition, however, is not able to accept the countering of the isolating effect of death by seeing it as a return from individuality to oneness with universal reality. Death, argues Alan Watts, far from being an isolating event, is the uncovering of one's identity with all that there is. Such an approach is incompatible with the Christian conviction of the true reality and importance of relationships and of the individual self as the subject of those relationships. But is not the assurance of the continuance of those relationships a falsity? Surely they are destroyed by death, unless we split man into a spiritual self or soul and a body which it uses temporarily; in other words, unless we make the individual self essentially bodiless, which would contradict the whole argument of this book.

I want to approach the problem by asking what it means to be an individual. On this question I have found most helpful an essay of Hans Jonas on "Biological Foundations of Individuality." Here is a passage in which he summarizes his account of the meaning of individual identity:

> Only those entities are individuals whose being is their own doing (and thus, in a sense, their task): entities, in other words, that are delivered up to their being for their being, so that their being is committed to them and they are committed to keeping up this being by ever renewed acts of it. Entities, therefore, which in their being are exposed to the alternative of not-being as potentially imminent, and achieve being in answer to this constant imminence; entities, therefore, that are temporal in their innermost nature, that have being only by ever becoming, with each moment posing a new issue in their history; whose *identity* over time is thus, not the inert one of a permanent substratum, but the self-created one of continuous performance; entities, finally, whose *difference* from the *other,* from the rest of things, is not adventitious and indifferent to them, but a dynamic attribute of their being, in that the tension of this difference is the very medium of each one's maintaining itself in its selfhood by standing off the other and communing with it at the same time.[16]

Individuality, in other words, is a self-creating, self-constituting performance, with individual identity and difference being the effect of an inner dynamic. Jonas sees those conditions as being verified only in organisms, so that individuality is grounded in the biological mode of being. He notes how the organism enjoys "a sort of *freedom* with respect to its own substance, an independence from that same matter of which it nonetheless wholly consists."[17] The elements of which a plant or animal is made may totally change in the metabolic process over a period, and yet the plant or animal remains identically the same. Further, the lesser integration of the animal into its environment, as compared to the plant, is a measure of greater individuality. To be self-constituting as an individual means *not to be* integrated with the world, and the greater the individuality, the greater the distance from the world.[18]

These considerations of Jonas may serve as a starting point for reflection upon human individuality and death. But what follows here is offered on my own responsibility and should not be attributed to Jonas himself.

The difficulty of using the concept of individuality as self-creation to suggest a continuance of the individual beyond death is that death is not something that we do, but something that happens to us. It is not part of the self-constituting process of our individuality. According to Kübler-Ross, the first reaction of people when learning of a terminal illness is denial: "No, not me, it cannot be true."[19] Some theologians are eager to present death as a human act in which one recapitulates one's whole life and makes a final choice. But to present death in the first place as a free human action, to forget that death is an event that overcomes us, is to be untrue to human experience. Death may be accepted in a human action, but it comes upon us from without, frequently filling us with a sense of untimeliness and waste.[20]

In passing, I should add here that I see no reason to use this general experience of death as not of our choosing, even when interpreted, with a conviction of divine providence in the external events of life, as an occasion for establishing a taboo against any voluntary acceleration or causing of death. The various issues involving death by choice are complex and require the most careful consideration and a discriminating moral judgment. All the same, I should agree with Daniel Maguire that there would seem to be instances where there are proportionate reasons to end life deliberately and where it is right to do so. And what is particularly relevant here, God's will concerning the death of an individual should not be identified with biological factors causing death.[21] But even in the case of the self-infliction of death, it is still inflicted; it is not in direct continuity with the self-constituting performance of our dynamic identity.

But is it then the simple destruction of that biologically grounded individual identity? In many ways it is. It is the end of a whole series of activities, which were creative of various levels of the self, and those levels of the self come to an end with the cutting short of those activities. The crucial question is whether part of the continuous performance which is our individual identity is activity that death does not bring to an end. John Dunne puts this point well:

> Everything depends on what life a man has in him before he dies. A woman's change of life is an image of death. If her life before the change contains little that is creative other than her fertility, then after the change she may seem only a ghost of the woman she was. If, on the contrary, there is some other creativity in her life, then her life after the change may still seem full and substantial. Something similar may happen at death. The change of life is the end of the fertility cycle; death is the end of all cycles. If nothing is going on in a man or a woman's life except the cycles of activity that death brings to an end, then after death there may be nothing left but a ghost of the former man or woman. If, on the contrary, something else is going on, something that would not have to come to a close with the cycles, then after death there may be some full and substantial existence.[22]

Christian belief in the continuance of individual identity beyond death would seem, then, to require a relationship with God as constitutive of the inmost self. This continues through death and becomes the basis for a new set of relationships with the world. A biological accident in plant or animal can bring a major shift in relationship to the environment and yet not destroy identity, so that there is continuity but only within a shattering dis-

continuity. So, analogously, death might be seen as a
biological accident for a person whose deepest identity is
a dynamic relationship with God. The continuous performance, which is his self-creative individuality, persists
though in a new mode.

Several points arise in connection with this interpretation. The biblical and Christian teaching that the conquest of death is a grace is represented here by making
the continuance of identity dependent upon a relationship with God as constituting the inmost self. If there is in
the person no relationship or activity which does not of its
nature terminate in death, there is no ground for the
continuance of individual identity. This indeed suggests
a theory of conditional immortality. The conclusion may
be unwelcome, but if human individual identity is the
self-creative process of an historical, embodied person, I
see no alternative. Any assertion of a universal, uncondi-
tional, individual immortality, possessed from conception, must rest on a questionable anthropology that de-
prives the human person of his historicalness or his bodiliness or of both. On the other hand, I should not myself
want to assert with any certitude the age at which a truly
human, and thus embodied, response to God might be
possible. As for those who freely refuse to actualize the
deeper levels of the self, the cessation of their stunted
selves at death would seem to be a defensible interpretation of the symbolism of hell.

Further, my interpretation does not agree with the
analysis of death as the separation of a spiritual soul from
a material body. The human person is inseparably
spiritual and material: the body is the pattern, the articulation, the expression, and the outward relationship of
the person; the spiritual self is the centeredness and
self-possession of the person. Death is a transition or
change affecting the whole person, but made visible in
the bodily destruction. Death, if and when individual
identity persists, is not the entry into a purely spiritual

state, but the beginning of a new relationship to the world, a new mode of bodiliness for the centered self. In brief, the centered self continues because it is grounded upon a relationship with God, and its essential bodiliness is realized on a new level and in a new manner as yet unknown to us.

Karl Rahner, in his book, *On the Theology of Death*,[23] has already expressed dissatisfaction with the model that depicts death as the separation of soul from body. He also suggests that death is the soul's "entrance into some deeper, all-embracing openness in which her cosmic relationship to the universe is more fully realized."[24] I do not find his further reflections on the "all-cosmic relationship" attained at death particularly illuminating, nor am I convinced that "all-cosmic" is the best designation of the new relationship; but I do agree that death is not the departure of a spiritual soul out of all relationship with the material universe.

The Christian belief in the resurrection of the body is for me a symbolic expression that life after death is the continuing individual identity of embodied persons in relation to one another and to this material universe. Any literal interpretation, which, for example, takes it as the reanimation of the corpse or its replacement by a similar body—"pickled in Spirit," to use Alan Watts' phrase,[25]— fall into the grotesque. Resurrection is, then, a state beginning at death, as the human self enters into its new mode of being and acting.

In order to show that the continuance of the individual identity of an embodied person beyond death is not entirely absurd and calling for dismissal at once as contradictory, appeal may be made, as I have suggested, to the independence of all organisms from the elements of which they consist at any one time. This independence is found even in plants and animals, but the degree of independence increases the higher the organism. It is therefore conceivable that in man this independence may, at least in some cases, become such that death is transcended analogously to a major biological accident. But that death is thus overcome is sheer hypothesis, unless there are further grounds for asserting it. Belief in life after death must rest, it seems to me, on the conviction that there is something going on in our lives which of its nature is indestructible by death.

So, the Christian belief in individual immortality rests upon the conviction that the personal relationship with God to which we are called would be rendered meaningless if thought of as cut off by death. It is the experience of relating to God, precisely as individuals in a loving interpersonal relationship, which grounds belief in personal survival of death. The same line of thought might be extended to other relationships. There are some relationships that so affect the very center of the personality that we can truly say that they would not be destroyed by the cessation of those activities that death brings to an end.

At this point the Christian view of death rejoins in its own way the Eastern view. In other words, death for Christians also is the uncovering of what is most real in human existence, the stripping off of what has no lasting value, and the manifestation of true, transphenomenal reality of the self. Death is not the transition to another life in no continuity with this present life, the replacement of life in this world for a better life in another world; it is the strengthening and deepening of a life that constitutes our essential identity here and now.

Death, then, may be the cessation of our identity if there is nothing in our lives that is not of its nature brought to an end at death. For death to become distinctively human, with the consequence of the continuance of individual identity, we must live in such a way that we may die in a hope that is founded on the presence of a transcendent dimension in the life we already have as persons. The art of living is thus the art of dying.

Although death is an event that happens to us, "to die" is an active verb, expressing something we do. Dying as an activity of ours may express what is going on at the unconscious level, or at least without our choice, as when "I am dying" expresses the onward course of a fatal disease within me. But the active verb "to die" may be extended in its meaning, as in Paul and other religious writers, so that it refers to the conscious acceptance of death and to a mode of living that anticipates death and allows its coming reality to have an impact upon present existence.

We may here adapt the five stages which Elisabeth Kübler-Ross[26] discovered in the reactions of terminally ill patients to the awareness of their impending death. These stages were denial, anger, bargaining, depression, and acceptance. Can we not see these stages of reaction to the news that we are now near death as recapitulating the phases of a lifelong struggle to come to terms with the finitude of present existence and to purify our hope from infantile desires?

First, we deny our death explicitly or implicitly. We hide from the fact of death and live as though we are never going to die. Then, usually, as life goes on and middle age makes clear the futility of most of our ambitions, we give way to feelings of anger, rage, envy, and resentment. The third or bargaining stage might well be represented by the vulgar forms of religious hope. We are like little children who think we can put off the inevitable if we promise to be very good. We pretend that death will not be the loss of the present form of our identity and experience. When self-deception does not endure, we pass into the next stage, depression. Eventually, if we come through this, we reach the final stage of acceptance. What corresponds, in the midst of living, to the quiet expectation and gradual breaking off of relationships described by Kübler-Ross is detachment.

Detachment during life is when we are open and

responsive to reality and other people in a manner that is self-transcending, self-forgetting. Its opposite is the possessiveness of an enclosed ego, trying to fill its emptiness, but refusing to feel. We are ready for death, we accept death, not when our lives are empty and restless with unsatisfied desires, but when they are rich because we live in an open responsiveness. I have said that the art of living is the art of dying. I must add that the art of dying is the art of living, and indeed of living to the full.

V.
The Inhumanity of Evil

If the Christian emphasis upon the individual is unique, so, too is the Christian Devil. Other religions have their demons or evil spirits, some even have a Devil, but no other religion has conceived so purely malignant a spirit, the personification of evil, as the Christian tradition. Christian belief in the Devil is bound up with the Christian attitude to evil; namely, the exclusion of all evil from God and the consequent refusal to accept evil in oneself. What is evil? What do we exclude from our self-acceptance? What do we project externally as the Devil? The theme of the Devil is closely linked to the theme of the self, the attitude to the body, the refusal or acceptance of feelings, openness to the world or withdrawal from it.

The chief issue, then, is the Christian understanding of evil. But the way must be cleared for a discussion of that issue by dealing briefly with some points that usually come to people's minds when the question of the Devil is raised. First, belief in spirits. Belief in spirits, usually

hostile or evil spirits, is almost universal among preliter-
ate peoples and is also found among the adherents of all
the major world religions. Personally I think that the rise
of empirical science has excluded any such belief for us
today. Or let me put it less emphatically: those who want
to combine belief in demons with an acceptance of science are guilty of inconsistency.

This is not because science has directly disproved the
existence of demons. It neither has nor can do that. It is
because belief in demons is the product of a prescientific
mentality. According to that mentality, everything out of
the way or contrary to what was usual or expected was
assigned to the activity of capricious spirits. These spirits
were responsible for a failure of crops, for injuries; for all
forms of sickness, disease, and death; and especially for
madness. Everything was given a personal dimension or
purpose, because no distinction was yet made between
things in their relation to us and things in the meaning
they had in themselves in their relation to one another.
Again, the prescientific mentality did not distinguish between fact and fiction, between what could be affirmed as
being so in reality and what was the imaginative expression of a personal response. Belief in demons was not,
therefore, a belief grounded upon a gathering and careful weighing of data and a testing of hypotheses; it was
simply an imaginative, spontaneous expression of the
personal impact of various occurrences.

There are two reasons for preferring the scientific to
the prescientific outlook in the question of the existence
of demons and similar matters. First, science already
gives a more useful and more coherent account of a wide
range of the phenomena previously attributed to demons. Few of us would prefer a witch doctor to a physi-
cian in ordinary illnesses. Even though science may be
baffled over some phenomena, it is more reasonable to
look to further research to extend its explanatory range
than to appeal to imaginative stories. Second, the theory

of knowledge behind the empirical method represents an advance in human self-consciousness by a reflective and critical appropriation of its mental operations, whereas prescientific consciousness is naíve and unreflective.

It is, in fact, anachronistic to raise the question of demons in a scientific manner and ask: Are there intelligent beings other than man who interfere in human events and with whom men may communicate? Belief in demons was never a scientific answer to a scientifically posed question. But if one does mix myth and science and put the question, the answer is without hesitation that there is as yet no evidence sufficient to support such an hypothesis. Parapsychological phenomena point to psychic forces not yet adequately known or studied, but they do not require any appeal to nonhuman intelligences. Possession symptoms likewise do not demand belief in demons for anyone who does not already accept their existence on other, religious, grounds.

However, belief in demons operates on two levels. The first level is the one I have been handling; namely, the question whether a certain type of being exists in the objective order. Nowadays, all such questions are answered by an empirical investigation of the data. As I have said, there is no adequate evidence for asserting the existence of demons. But to approach belief in demons simply on that level is to miss the point. There is a second level: people who believed in demons did so because it was a symbolic expression of various elements in human existence and experience.

At this point a further distinction is required. The almost universally widespread belief in demons symbolically expresses merely men's sense of the seemingly capricious and hostile features of the world in which they live. It does not run deep. When, however, we turn to the Devil of the Christian tradition we come to a belief of a different order. In the figure of Satan or the Devil,

Christians are asserting the reality of a totally malignant spirit of cosmic evil. There is, they believe, a kingdom of evil, hell, ruled over by the Devil, with countless spirits as subjects, everlastingly damned. The Devil and his servants rage through this world, seeking to destroy men and bring them into the kingdom of evil. Men find themselves between two kingdoms, and on their free choice, on divine predestination, or on some combination of both depends whether they will enjoy eternal happiness in heaven or be tortured everlastingly in the fiery pit of hell.

But before more is said about the symbolic meaning of the Christian Devil, a second preliminary point must be disposed of: diabolic possession. Granted the exaggerations of popular accounts, there is still more than enough evidence to put the occurrence of paranormal phenomena beyond doubt in many instances of so-called possession by the Devil. What are we to make of these phenomena? While I do not think that all of them can be explained as psychosomatic disorders, I do hold that much that is associated with diabolic possession may be explained in that way.

I have already quoted *The Primal Scream,* the account of primal therapy by its inaugurator, Arthur Janov.[1] Janov, it will be remembered, explains neurosis as due to the repression of primal pain; namely, a pain so intolerable for a child that the child exposed to it shuts off the reality of its own needs and desires and defends itself by hiding behind an unreal or neurotic self. Locked up in each neurotic, Janov argues, is a pool of primal pain, and for the cure of the neurosis that pain must be released by being actually felt. It must be felt, not just known. The pain—caused, for example, by the lack of a warm, affectionate father—which the child refused to feel in childhood must be unlocked and felt fully. Primal therapy is designed to release the pain. The release takes place in the overwhelming experience of the primal scream.

Janov describes the incident that led him to the discovery of primal pain as the cause of neurosis. Danny Wilson was a twenty-two-year-old college student, withdrawn, sensitive, quiet. In a therapy session, for reasons that were not clear to himself, Janov was moved to ask him to call out, "Mommy! Daddy!" and, when Danny at first refused, to insist. Finally, Danny gave in and started to call out. Janov records the incident:

> As he began, he became noticeably upset. Suddenly he was writhing on the floor in agony. His breathing was rapid, spasmodic; "Mommy! Daddy!" came out of his mouth almost involuntarily in loud screeches. He appeared to be in a coma or hynoptic state. The writhing gave way to small convulsions and finally he released a piercing, deathlike scream that rattled the walls of my office. The entire episode lasted only a few minutes, and neither Danny nor I had any idea what had happened. All he could say afterward was: "I made it! I don't know what, but I can *feel*."[2]

Once Janov had worked out the theory and technique of primal therapy, he was to witness many such outrushes of primal pain, with physical contortions and violent expressions of suppressed anger and hatred. Further, the cures led to remarkable physical changes in patients, such as the disappearance of many psychosomatic disorders and even physical growth in persons underdeveloped in some respect.

I have referred to primal therapy because some of the scenes described in Janov's account of it resemble what is reported from exorcisms of possessed persons. Provided, then, we do not think that all cases of possession have the dramatic accumulation of symptoms found in popular accounts like *The Exorcist,* and are also willing to admit the ineffectiveness of much conventional psychiatry and psychotherapy, we can reasonably look to present science for explanations of a great deal that is reported as diabolical possession.

All the same, not all the phenomena can be accounted for within the limits of present science. Some occurrences, such as psychokinesis and xenoglossolalia, are in the category of what is usually called the parapsychological. Although the study of parapsychology is being increasingly recognized as a serious and important intellectual enterprise, it is still not fully accepted by the scientific establishment. But it seems to me that the more intelligent and more reasonably grounded response to the paranormal is to work for a widening of the concepts and methods of empirical science to deal with presently unacknowledged psychic forces rather than to suppose the existence and activity of devils.

To turn now to the Christian Devil in its symbolic functioning. The Devil of Christian belief enters deeply into the Christian outlook on the world and human life. It is a symbol that sin or evil is taken with ultimate or eternal seriousness. But first some points of a comparative nature.

The demons of the Hindu religious tradition are marginal in relation to the central meaning and life of that tradition. They are merely elements of popular mythology and culture, in that sense secular in character, taken up into the religious synthesis. Moreover, they are never devils in the Western sense, even if they are depicted as hideous, because they represent aspects of nature, features of universal reality, not sin.

The Buddhist tradition did develop the symbol of Māra, the Evil One, which is strikingly parallel to the Satan of the New Testament.[3] Both represent a religious remoulding of popular, quasi-secular demonology. In both instances the religious treatment has replaced the unordered pluralism of many demons with a single, unified symbol; though in neither case is this achieved completely, because each principal figure has its attendant host of devils. The difference between Māra and the Satan of the New Testament is that Satan stands for the evils found in human society and its institutions, the corrupting pressure of the evils in man's corporate life, whereas Māra symbolizes all that makes an impact upon the individual from without, the whole of *samsāra* as Buddhism conceives it.

In Israel, demonology was virtually excluded by the prophets, who insisted upon looking inward to man's heart rather than outward to the environment for the source of man's troubles. They also associated demons with false gods. But later in the apocalyptic literature there was a reassertion of demonology, together with a movement, as in Buddhism, toward a unitary conception of the evil forces. Thus Satan emerged as a single, supreme enemy of God. An early stage in that development is the figure of Satan in the Book of Job, where he is not the Devil of later teaching but an adversary or counsel for the prosecution, present before God in the court of heaven, but yet the cause of unmerited suffering. In the New Testament, Satan represents a late stage in the apocalyptic development, which forms its background.

So, we find the single figure of the Evil One as a religious symbol formed out of a folk demonology in Buddhism, in Judaism, in Christianity, and, we may add, in Islam. The Christian tradition, however, experienced an emphasis upon the Devil altogether exceptional in the horror of its expressions and in the impact it had upon attitudes and behavior. Why?

With much plausibility, Alan Watts argues that belief in the Devil in its later Christian form is the final consequence of ethical monotheism, namely the exclusion of all evil from God and the absolutizing of good.[4] In other religions, good and evil form a polarity, one of the many polarities among the relativities of this phenomenal world. The Absolute is beyond good and evil, and neither good nor evil as men conceive them are absolutized. For example, in Hindu imagery, Shiva in his dance, the dance of the universe, is depicted as surrounded with flames, flashing with terror, but one of his many hands is held upright with the palm open to the spectator, the gesture meaning, "Fear not." In other words, the terror is part of the play or dance or magical illusion (*maya*) of the universe. Evil appears as one of the many masks of God.[5]

What was the origin of ethical monotheism? In Persia, Zoroastrianism developed as an explicitly dualistic religion, with two ultimate principles of good and evil. Originally, even here the two principles were brothers or twins, and thus seen as having a common root. But it did become a dualism, the first religion to absolutize the good, even though this meant also absolutizing evil. Probably under the influence of Zoroastrianism from the fifth century onward, the later Hebrew prophets, while refusing dualism, met the challenge it posed by developing ethical monotheism, thus seeing the universe as governed by a single, purely beneficent God, with all evil attributed to the rebellion of men against God.

We have already seen that the prophetic exclusion of demonology and the attribution of all evil to men did not last. The revival of demonology in the context of ethical monotheism led to the prominence of Satan as the personification of evil. He was the original rebel, to whom all evil was attributed. But the more his rebellion was denounced and implacably resisted, the more he himself, the rebel, became endowed with godlike power. Thus Satan, in his proud defiance of God, becomes himself a god.

In Christianity the dualism implicit in ethical monotheism came out into the open in its depiction of the Devil and its stress upon sin and hell. Because the Christian God refuses his shadow side and identifies himself with unalloyed goodness, the Devil emerges as God's unconsciously produced shadow. When Christians absolutize moral goodness, they are led to attribute ultimate seriousness to sin and evil. Hell becomes the counterpart of Heaven, the everlasting bliss of the just has its correlative in the everlasting torments of the wicked. The mystery of iniquity is placed alongside the mystery of goodness.

That has considerable repercussions on the way we think of ourselves and consequently live. If we take the polarity of good and evil as we find them in human existence, and then identify God the Absolute with a goodness excluding evil, we make it impossible for us to accept ourselves radically. Instead of the radical self-acceptance required for a fully human life, the groundwork of our lives, of our thought and action, becomes anxiety; that is, the sense and terror of being ultimately wrong, the feeling that we are basically corrupt. Viewed from that standpoint, Satan is in effect human evil projected externally and refused integration. The Devil represents all that we will not acknowledge in ourselves. The inhumanity of evil—yes! because when human evil is disowned, it becomes terrifyingly inhuman.

Although the Devil as the implacable adversary of God and man appears in the New Testament and early Christian writings, it is not until the late Middle Ages, the fourteenth century, that demonography was fully developed and the malignant image of the Devil was portrayed in all its horror. In that connection it has been observed that the emergence of the Devil image in its full repulsiveness is linked with the wave of sadistic lust that swept over Europe and showed itself in the torturing and burning of witches and heretics. The figure of the Devil is, after all, that of the lustful Pan, and his attendant demons are satyrs. Demonography is in fact a scarcely concealed pornography. The monstrous Devil is the external caricature, the magnified image of the erotic, animal, self-seeking, and other features of human life which men constantly refuse to acknowledge and accept.[6]

The fascination of people with Satan and the diabolical is the attraction of what in mild cases is simply alien, chaotic, frightening because as yet unassimilated, unin-

tegrated; and of what in severe cases is hateful yet allur-
ing because a rejected and repressed part of themselves.
Satan is thus the human become inhuman because projected externally and in that way made monstrous.

The process, however, leads to truly hideous and re-
volting effects when the projection falls not simply upon
an image or symbolic figure, but upon other people identified with the symbol. So, in the course of Christian
history, alien people have been seen as children of the
Devil or at least under his domination; alien religions
have been interpreted as Devil-worship; witches and
heretics have been burnt as instruments of the Devil. The
virulent anti-Semitism of the fourth-century saint, John
Chrysostom, associates the Jews with the Devil. "Men
possessed by the devil," he calls them. "They murder
their offspring and immolate them to the devil" is his
accusation. He describes the synagogue as "the domicile
of the devil" and "a cavern of devils."[7] The same process
continues even when reference to the Devil is dropped.
The Jews in Nazi Germany became the receptacle of all
the evil the Germans would not acknowledge in themselves. Commentators on the situation in South Africa
argue convincingly with much evidence that the white
South Africans have made the blacks the symbol of a side
of their nature they are denying.

Satan is thus a symbol of what we disown in ourselves. That explains the fascination of the Evil One. But
we must, as Jung urges, "integrate the Evil One."[8] When
human evil is externalized and refused acknowledgement, it becomes monstrous. The instances we think of as
diabolical evil, such as Dachau and Auschwitz, are instances where the evil is inhuman, not because it comes
from a nonhuman agent; it is inhuman because perpe-
trated by men who have denied their own humanity.

What does all this mean for our image of God? I will
return to this point in a moment. First, however, I want to
argue that not all use of the symbol of Satan is unhealthy.

The figure of the Devil also expresses a continuing and inescapable feature of the human condition. The New Testament is helpful here. Certainly, it reproduces the general belief of its day in demons; but this is just a reflection of a past culture and is of no particular religious significance. The case is different when we look at the references, not to demons in general, but to Satan or the Devil. Only in one of the late books of the New Testament, the Book of Revelation or the Apocalypse, is Satan placed in an unresolvable enmity with God—a final, implacable, eternal enmity. In earlier writings Satan represents spiritual evil, but a spiritual evil that will be overcome.

Trevor Ling in his study, *The Significance of Satan: New Testament Demonology and its Contemporary Relevance,*[9] shows by a close examination of the texts that both the sayings of Jesus and the writings of Paul shift attention away from demons to the single figure of Satan. Moreover, the Satan of the New Testament, he argues, derives his power ultimately from men themselves. Satan represents the evil that dominates the world of men apart from Christ. This is how he sums up the meaning of the symbol: Satan is "the spirit of unredeemed man's collective life, that which dominates the individual, and stifles his growth in truly personal life; a spirit, moreover, which is characterized by a constant effort towards self-deification."[10]

That interpretation corresponds in part to what Paul Ricoeur, the French phenomenologist, wrote in his masterly study, *The Symbolism of Evil.* In discussing the myth of Adam and the serpent, he says:

> ". . . the serpent represents the following situation: in the historical experience of man, every individual finds evil *already there;* nobody begins it absolutely. If Adam is not the first man, in the naively temporal sense of the word, but the typical man, he can symbolize both the experience of the "beginning" of humanity with each individual and

the experience of the "succession" of men. Evil is part of the interhuman relationship, like language, tools, institutions; it is transmitted; it is tradition, and not only something that happens. There is thus an anteriority of evil to itself, as if evil were that which always precedes itself, that which each man finds and continues while beginning it, but beginning it in his turn. That is why, in the Garden of Eden, the serpent is already there; he is the other side of that which begins."[11]

In other words, we need the symbol of Satan or its equivalent because we cannot exhaustively explain evil in terms of personal guilt. Evil precedes each one of us. Before our personal conscience has developed, we are caught up in a social network of cumulative sin. When we awake to sin, we are already participants in situations of injustice, hatred, prejudice, lust, and so on. Personal sin in that way becomes a yielding to the temptation of Satan; namely, a yielding or consent to the already existing tradition of evil in which we find ourselves. No individualistic account of morality is enough. Eliminate Satan or the cumulative social tradition of evil, and men will ignore social evils for which they do not consider themselves personally responsible. We have to fight Satan or struggle with an evil that precedes us and tempts us to compromise with it.

There is further matter for reflection in the myth of Adam and his sin. Ricoeur rightly sees it as coming out of ethical monotheism. He compares it to the other myths of the beginning and end of evil; namely, the struggle with chaos in the drama of creation in theogonic myths, the tragic myths involving the theology of the god who tempts, blinds, and leads astray; and the myth of the exiled soul, which divides man into soul and body. Unlike those, the myth of Adam is concerned to establish the innocence of God. As Ricoeur says:

Hebrew monotheism, and more particularly the ethical character of that monotheism, undermined theogony and the tragic god, who is still theogonic, and made them impossible. . . . The purely anthropological conception of the origin of evil is the counterpart of this general "de-mythologization" of theogony; *because* "Yahweh reigns by his Word," because "God is Holy," evil must enter into the world by a sort of catastrophe in the created. . . . The Adamic myth is the fruit of the prophetic accusation directed against man; the same theology that makes God innocent accuses man.[12]

It is noteworthy, however, that the myth does not succeed in presenting a purely human origin of evil. There is the serpent. Besides, like Satan, representing evil as external to the individual because found embodied in a cumulative social tradition, the serpent symbolizes, it seems, an even more radical externality of evil, namely, evil as a cosmic structure. The serpent is more than the excess of human sin over the sins of human individuals; the serpent is the Adversary, "the pole of a counterparticipation,"[13] namely, a source of iniquity beyond man.

Thus, the ethical vision of reality is one-sided. We cannot absolutize moral goodness. Ricoeur writes:

This "ethicization" of man and God tends toward a moral vision of the world according to which History is a tribunal, pleasures and pains are retribution, God himself is a judge. At the same time, the whole of human experience assumes a penal character. Now, this moral vision of the world was wrecked by Jewish thought itself when it meditated on the suffering of the innocent. The Book of Job is the upsetting document that records this shattering of the moral vision of the world. The figure of Job bears witness to the irreducibility of the evil of scandal to the evil of fault, at least on the scale of human experience; the theory of retribution, which was the first naive expression of the moral vision of the world, does not account for all the unhappiness of the world.[14]

There is indeed a hyperethical dimension to evil.

Evil is not reducible to human fault. The inhumanity of
evil! If we are wrong to project human evil externally and
by disowning it to make it inhumanly monstrous, we are
also mistaken if we attempt to attribute all evil to man's
sinning and find its origin in man's conscious fault. Good
and evil form a polarity in reality, and we cannot absolutize either pole in isolation from the other. God as
Absolute is the coincidence of opposites, the transcend-
ing of the polarities, beyond good and evil.

That does not mean the abolition of ethical distinctions. As Alan Watts puts it apropos of the related question of self-acceptance:

> The fear that self-acceptance necessarily annihilates ethi-
> cal judgement is groundless, for we are perfectly able to
> distinguish between up and down at any point on the
> earth's surface, realizing at the same time that there is no
> up and down in the larger framework of the cosmos.[15]

Nor, therefore, does it mean losing the insights of
ethical monotheism concerning the love and justice of
God. To admit the polarity does not imply a denial that
good is the positive, evil the negative. But it does mean
acknowledging the limitations of our human concept of
the good and thus tempering our moral indignation. As
Ricoeur puts it:

> The myth of the fall needs those other myths, so that the
> ethical God it presupposes may continue to be a *Deus
> Absconditus* and so that the guilty man it denounces may
> also appear as the victim of a mystery of iniquity which
> makes him deserving of Pity as well as of Wrath.[16]

It was the absolutizing of the good as we conceive it
that led to the absolutizing of evil. But as a matter of fact,
both good and evil when absolutized become monstrous.
There is often little to choose between the conception of
the Devil and some concepts of the All-Good, All-Just,
Omnipotent God of Wrath, the Judge of mankind. Men

have been slaughtered in the name of the good God as men have conceived him.

In his book, *The God of Evil*, Frederick Sontag writes: *"The flaws which lead to man's downfall must find their source in God's nature or else go unexplained.* The same tendencies in man, those in which nonbeing both reveals and threatens his existence, must be present at the root of the divine nature."[17] The same thrust toward a deeper conception of God is set forth more imaginatively in the novel *Incognito* by the Rumanian writer, Petru Dumitriu. The hero undergoes the wretched experience of a political prisoner in a totalitarian state. In and through that experience he learns to recognize God in everything, including evil. It is impossible to convey the impact of a powerful novel by a few quotations, but these may serve to indicate the theme of God present *incognito* at the heart of all things:

> Yes, He is perfect, but He is also terrible and evil. He is both perfect and imperfect. He is all things, and He confines himself to none.[18]

> God is everything. He is also composed of volcanoes, cancerous growths and tapeworms. But if you think that justifies you in jumping into the crater of an active volcano, or wallowing in despair and crime and death, or inoculating yourself with a virus—well go ahead. You're like a fish that asks, 'Do you mean to say God isn't only water, He's dry land as well?' To which the answer is, 'Yes, my dear fish, He's dry land as well, but if you go climbing on to dry land you'll be sorry'.[19]

> What is difficult is to love the world as it is now, while it is doing what it is doing to me, and causing those nearest to me to suffer, and so many others. What is difficult is to bless the material world which contains the Central Committee and the Securisti; to love and pardon them. Even to bless them, for they are one of the faces of God, terrifying and sad.[20]

To sum up: Satan is the counterpart of our image of ourselves and our image of God, both images being related. When there is a large measure of self-acceptance, the figure of Satan is not terrifying, but tends toward humor and buffoonery, representing all that is strange, chaotic, and, as yet, unintegrated. But Satan becomes an image of horror and hatred, repulsive yet fascinating, when he represents elements in our humanity that we disown and repress. Likewise when God is formed in the image of a self-righteous monarch, cut off from all the pain and suffering, the frailty and sin of this world, personified moral goodness made absolute, relentlessly at enmity with all evil, then Satan becomes the personification of evil and hatred made absolute, his kingdom a place of refined and everlasting torment where the pain and malice of the universe, unalloyed and intensified, is made ultimate and eternal. When God, however, is the mysterious and unknown Reality present in everything as its origin and inmost being, then Satan, though terrifying, is but one of the many masks of God. To recognize this is to be able to sing with the Easter hymn: "O truly necessary sin of Adam which the death of Christ has blotted out! O happy fault which merited such and so great a Redeemer." And again, to say with Juliana of Norwich, the fourteenth-century mystic, as quoted by T. S. Eliot:

> Sin is Behovely, but
> All shall be well, and
> All manner of thing shall be well.[21]

VI.
Sex: Love and Sin

William Empson in his book, *Milton's God,* makes a fierce attack upon the Christian God as "the wickedest thing yet invented by the black heart of man."[1] His chief reason is the sadistic delight Christians attribute to their God in the infliction of punishment upon the damned. He links that conception of God with the Christian horror of sex.

We need not yield to the extreme of Empson's attack to acknowledge that a Christian denial of sex is at the source of many of the unpleasant features of Western Christian history, with its intolerance and violence. It was another point that struck me most in Empson's account. He remarks upon the inconsistency between the Christian attitude to sex and the insistence of the Christian religion upon the unique value of love.[2] Like Empson, I also find a contradiction there. It shows itself in an acute fashion when Christian mystics take sexual love as a symbol of the loving union of the soul with God. A fear and denigration of sexual love, or at best a quiet ignoring of its fleshly reality, is joined to its use as an image of supreme loving.

Origen's commentary on the Song of Songs, though not the first Christian commentary on the Hebrew love song, is, because of its quality, considered "the first great work of Christian mysticism."[3] But while he wants to use the bridal embrace as a symbol of the spiritual union of the soul and Christ, he is afraid from the beginning that the imagery is going to cause "carnal" thoughts:

> But if any man who lives only after the flesh should approach it, to such a one the reading of this Scripture will be the occasion of no small hazard and danger. For he, not knowing how to hear love's language in purity and with chaste ears, will twist the whole manner of his hearing of it away from the inner spiritual man on to the outward and carnal; and he will be turned away from the spirit to the flesh, and will foster carnal desires in himself, and it will seem to be the Divine Scriptures that are thus urging and egging him on to fleshly lust.

> For this reason, therefore, I advise and counsel everyone who is not yet rid of the vexations of flesh and blood and has not ceased to feel the passion of his bodily nature, to refrain completely from reading this little book and the things that will be said about it.[4]

Origen in no way recognizes that sexual love is able to serve as a symbol of mystical union because, in its very reality as a bodily, erotic spontaneity, it has a self-transcending power, leading the human self out of an egocentric isolation to embrace, spiritually as well as bodily, the reality of another person. His fear of sex prevents him from seeing that the erotic dynamism of bodily love is not an arbitrary and somewhat bold and dangerous symbol, but an intrinsic element in the movement of an embodied person in openness toward the plenitude of reality, toward God. Instead, the symbol is rendered abstract and formal, almost purely literary, on the overt level, while one suspects its religious use is operating latently as a substitute and disguise for unacknowledged feelings.

How different the fearful, passionless tones of Origen from the rich sensuousness of the Song of Songs itself!

> How graceful are your feet in sandals,
> O queenly maiden!
> Your rounded thighs are like jewels,
> the work of a master hand.
> Your navel is a rounded bowl
> that never lacks mixed wine.
> Your belly is a heap of wheat,
> encircled with lilies.
> Your two breasts are like two fawns,
> twins of a gazelle.
> Your neck is like an ivory tower.
> Your eyes are pools in Heshbou,
> by the gate of Bath-rabbim.
> Your nose is like a tower of Lebanon,
> overlooking Damascus.
> Your head crowns you like Carmel,
> and your flowing locks are like purple;
> a king is held captive in the tresses.
>
> How fair and pleasant you are,
> O loved one, delectable maiden!
> You are stately as a palm tree,
> and your breasts are like its clusters.
> I say I will climb the palm tree
> and lay hold of its branches.
> Oh, may your breasts be like clusters of the vine,
> and the scent of your breath like apples,
> and your kisses like the best wine
> that goes down smoothly,
> gliding over lips and teeth.
>
> Song 7:1-9

Or, again, contrast Origen's fear of arousing carnal desires with the uninhibited vitality of this Vaishnava devotional lyric, expressing the love of Rādhā, who symbolizes the devotee of God, for the Lord Krishna:

> How beautiful the deliberate, sensuous union of the two:
> the girl playing this time the active role,

riding her lover's outstretched body in delight;
her smiling lips shine with drops of sweat; the god of love
offering pearls to the moon.
She of beautiful face hotly kisses the mouth of her beloved; the moon, with face bent down, drinks
of the lotus.
The garland hanging on her heavy breasts seems like a
stream of milk from golden jars.
The tinkling bells which decorate her hips sound the
triumphal music of the god of love.[5]

The language of the Christian mystics is frequently
erotic. Here is one example from John of the Cross:

Oh, night that guided me, Oh, night more lovely than the
dawn,
Oh, night that joined Beloved with Lover, Lover trans-
formed in the Beloved!
Upon my flowery breast. Kept wholly for himself alone,
There he stayed sleeping, and I caressed him, And the
fanning of the cedars made a breeze.
The breeze blew from the turret. As I parted his locks;
With his gentle hand he wounded my neck. And caused
all my senses to be suspended.
I remained, lost in oblivion; My face I reclined on the
Beloved.
All ceased and I abandoned myself, Leaving my cares
forgotten among the lilies.[6]

I see no reason to be in the least defensive about such
eroticism in itself. The love of a person for God is not
discontinuous with the love of that person for other
human persons. Since indeed God cannot be apprehended as an object, the love of God arises in us only
as a vista, an endlessly receding horizon, beyond some
human love. It is the transcendent dynamic in human
love itself that makes it appropriate to speak of love of
God. So, without the reality of human love, love of God
would have no meaning. What makes human love pecu-
liarly suitable as a vehicle for our relationship with God
is its power to break out of the limited framework of par-

ticular laws, institutions, and customs; to shatter the individual's carefully worked out plans and schemes; to take the person beyond himself and the world he has constructed for himself. But that disruptive yet liberating power of human love is most evident in the eros of human sexual love, as the love poetry and love songs of the world proclaim. The very untamed force that is feared in sexual love, namely, its power to make a man or woman give up everything for the person loved, makes it a movement out of the humanly constructed world toward God. For where the sexual love of another person is genuine and not simulated, where the person is indeed in love, not engaged in calculated seduction for sensual ends, the love is not self-centered, but a movement of the person beyond the ego and its narrow world.

Why, then, should not the mystics celebrate their love of God in erotic language and images? All would be well, but for the underlying Christian attitude toward sex. There are grounds for hesitation where sexual symbolism is used but the reality of sexual love is repressed. I cannot think it healthy psychologically to use imaginary sex as an expression of divine love, while sex in its bodily reality is rejected as the work of sin, or, at best, an obstacle to union with God. There is nothing unhealthy in an eroticism that sees in sexual love a dynamic that both expresses and mediates man's highest aspirations as a bodily person. But there is something unhealthy and corrupt in an eroticism that shrinks from the reality of sex while using its language and imagery.

There are two opposing ways in which symbols may function in our conscious life. They may be a flight from reality; in that case they serve as a substitute for feeling. They are a way of acting out needs, desires, sensations, and emotions one does not allow oneself to feel. For that reason, symbols are a sign of a divided self; they are inauthentic as the product of an unreal self. Since Freud, people have become aware of the "symbolic" meaning, in that sense, of various actions and forms of language. Such symbols are the indirect expression of what we resist directly confronting; and we no longer need that kind of symbolic language and behavior when we accept what was being repressed and then released symbolically. Religious symbols often function in that indirect fashion. Hence, the sound reasons for suspecting the eroticism of religious images and language when sexual feelings are rejected or unacknowledged.

But symbols may function in a different manner. They are, then, feelings made explicit and conscious. Feelings, as I have already argued, are not the movement of a self-enclosed subjectivity, but the response of the self-being of the subject to reality and values independent of itself. Feelings are the result of a connaturality between the subject and objective reality. Consequently, they come to expression in a conscious relationship of mutual participation between the subject and objects. In that mutual participation, while the subject vibrates to the reality of the object, the object in its turn represents the movement of the human spirit and embodies human meaning. Thus, once the current of feeling flows freely, symbols cease to be an acting out of what remains unfelt and become the transparency of actions and things to the meaning embodied in feelings and shared by their objects. Symbols, in that sense, are not a substitute for reality, but reality itself as responded to or felt, as expressive, as dynamic.

Sexual love, then, made into a symbol of divine love, may be a fantasy replacing the reality of sexual love itself. This makes divine love a phantasmal creation, to be left behind as one grows toward maturity and health. But sexual love as a symbol for divine love may be the very reality of sexual love when rendered transparent in its meaning as the embodiment and expression, the felt dynamism of the love of God.

We come back, therefore, to the inconsistency between the Christian emphasis upon love as the chief reality and concept in our religious and moral life and the strong presence in Christian history of a negative attitude to sex. Because of the complex medley of elements that entered into the formation of Western culture in relation to sex and marriage, there is no simple explanation of the inconsistency.[7] My interest here, however, is not with an historical explanation, but with finding a viable attitude to sexual love in the light of the insights concerning feeling I am setting forth in this book.

Prominent in the traditional Christian attitude, at both its best and worst, has been the desire for rational control of what is deemed to be a most rebellious instinct. This is still evident, amusingly so, in those modern Christian writers who are gingerly questioning whether, say, premarital sex is always sinful. They make a great point of insisting upon "responsible sex," fearful lest the sexual impulse should get out of control if the traditional absolute prohibitions should be relaxed.

An instance of the preoccupation with control is the presentation of sex in the writings of the Christian apologist, C. S. Lewis. It is fair to take him as an example because he has written a perceptive and much read book upon the different forms of love.[8] In an earlier work, *Mere Christianity*, he declares that the Christian rule limiting sex to monogamous marriage "is so difficult and so contrary to our instincts, that obviously either Christianity is wrong or our sexual instinct, as it now is, has gone wrong."[9] Naturally, he maintains that it is the instinct that has gone wrong. He goes on to refer to the burlesque act of striptease as confirming his contention that the sexual instinct in its present state is corrupt. "Now suppose you came to a country where you could fill a theatre by simply bringing a covered plate on to the stage and then slowly lifting the cover so as to let everyone see, just before the lights went out, ... Would you not think that in that country something had gone wrong with the appetite for food?" So, too, he maintains, striptease would indicate to anyone who had grown up in another world that something had gone wrong with the sexual instinct among us.[10]

Readers of Lewis's science fiction will remember how he makes use of his conviction about the corruption of man's sexual instinct in *Out of the Silent Planet*. There he depicts the *hrossa* on Malacandra or Mars as naturally continent, as experiencing sexual love and pleasure in an orderly fashion that instinctively limited the exercise of sex to the short period required for procreation. Man's unbridled sexuality is made to stand out in contrast as a puzzling aberration. As Ransom pondered:

> . . . at last it dawned upon him that it was not they, but his own species, that were the puzzle. That the *hrossa* should have such instincts was mildly surprising; but how came it that the instincts of the *hrossa* so closely resembled the unattained ideals of that far-divided species Man whose instincts were so deplorably different? What was the history of Man?[11]

The same conception of sex as an appetite that must be brought under control is found in another of his books, *The Great Divorce*. When one of the Ghosts allows the Angel to kill his lust, represented by a lizard, it turns into a magnificent stallion, ridden by him as master.[12] "Horse and master," a powerful animal at last fully under human control, is Lewis's vision of sex transformed.

I find Lewis's presentation of sexuality unsatisfactory in several respects. First, he unduly restricts the meaning of the sexual instinct. For me it is in no sense a human ideal that sexual love should be bounded by the narrow needs of procreation. Are we simply engaged in self-deception or, at best, doing what we can with a corrupted instinct when we give our sexuality a meaning ranging beyond the needs of begetting children? I think not. But there is little need to argue a point conceded today even by Catholic theologians. Again, Lewis makes absolute what he gives as the Christian rule: "Either marriage, with complete faithfulness to your partner, or else total abstinence."[13] For that reason he ignores the possibility of there being any meaning other than lust in whatever sexual manifestations run contrary to that rule. But, because human spontaneity, no more in the sexual sphere than elsewhere, exactly corresponds to the planned rational order of laws and institutions, that does not make its unordered manifestations lust. It is not lack of control that turns sensuousness into lust or sensuality, but the subordination of human bodily spontaneity to the egocentric drives of the human mind. Thus, with all sound sex rigidly tied to procreation and to the institution of monogamous marriage, Lewis depicts human beings as they actually are as being subjected to lustful urges to an extent only explicable by an inherited corruption of the sexual instinct. He thus repeats the dualistic and psychologically false model which sees the body as a set of rebellious impulses to be brought under control by the rational will.

I have in a previous chapter given my reasons in detail for rejecting that model for the understanding of men and women, even in their present disordered situation. It remains to apply explicitly to sexuality the attitude to the body I have already expounded.

The whole of bodily experience is sexual, because sexual differentiation affects it in its totality. That does not mean that the quality given to particular experiences by maleness or femaleness is necessarily of notable, let alone of determining, importance. For example, an aesthetic experience of a poem or painting in a man will always have some difference of tone from a similar experience in a woman, but what the two experiences have in common may be far more important than their difference. In other circumstances or experiences the difference due to sex may be of decisive value; it is usually so in personal relationships.

However, whether sexual differentiation is of great or little importance in particular experiences, because sex is all-pervasive, any malaise in persons about sex or about their maleness or femaleness and its implications will send its ripples throughout their human experience and have a distorting effect upon their feelings as a whole, namely, upon their responsiveness to reality. If there is to be a rich and genuine human responsiveness to reality in feeling; an openness to the joys and delights, the pain, suffering, and stress of human bodily experience; and an ability to relate to others in a free communication; then there must be a basic acceptance of sexuality and of the tone and quality with which it marks the totality of human living. This basic acceptance implies being in harmony and at ease with manifestations of sex more specific than the sexual coloring of all human experience.

Sex, in the more specific sense, is that feeling response to another person that makes one desire to weld that person's life and one's own into a common life, with a total sharing both bodily and spiritual. One yearns for the other as for a lost part of oneself, with a longing to merge oneself and one's life with the other into a single person and a single life. If the initial response is taken up and becomes mutual, then living sexually is the gradual realization of the desire for a unity of existence. Once begun, the working out of the relationship requires time and is often painful. It may prove impossible of completion, so that the attempt is best abandoned. It may, though possible of fulfillment or even basically completed, be broken off and destroyed. But when established and still moving toward greater realization, it brings a joyful richness of feeling that at one and the same time enhances everything else and makes everything else seem unimportant by comparison.

While the experience of falling in love may of itself bring a surge of personal growth, genuine eros or sexual love is only possible where there is a degree of maturity. That longing for the other as a lost part of oneself is not the same as the desire to possess another in order to fill one's own emptiness. True sexual love requires two adult persons who are not seriously deficient in self-being or self-knowledge and who are in touch with their own feelings and secure in their own self-image.

Sexual love, then, is not a remedy for an inadequacy of the self in its individual being, but a going beyond the individual self once securely established. That is why the intrinsic dynamism of sexual love is powerful in overcoming the tendency of the self to enclose itself upon itself in egocentric isolation. It is a liberation of the person from the gravity of self-concern, from the tendency to remain firmly within the orbit of the self and its limited world.

The same dynamism that gives the couple the ability to soar beyond the self in their own union will continue, if not checked, to carry the two beyond themselves, and their household *à deux* to other people and, in all and yet beyond all, to God. Sexual love is of its nature a symbol of union with God, because for bodily persons it is a liberating force that leads to God.

Sexual love is also a response of the total person to another. It has that wholeness, uniting bodily and spiritual, emotional and intelligent factors in a unified affection, which I described in discussing feelings. Hence, falling in love can have an integrating effect upon the person, healing the division in the self that results in sensuality or unfeeling rationality. All the same, granted its healing power, it essentially presupposes an integrated person. One must say again that sexual love is a surpassing of the individual self, not a remedy for the defects of individual growth. But because it is a feeling response of great richness, sexual love, if genuinely accepted and lived, prevents the person from ignoring the role of feeling in the apprehension of values and from succumbing to a onesided rationalism or positivism. It thus opens the way for the response to God in religious feeling.[14]

Other forms of human love, though often deep and sometimes more lasting than many instances of sexual love, do not bring the same yearning to blend personalities and lives into an intimate and complete unity. Thus, parental love moves toward the separation of the lives of the children from that of the parents. Friendship is nearest to sexual love, yet though grounded upon common interests and affinities of character, it is a relationship between people who keep their separate lives. Nevertheless, it would be wrong to make a clear and firm division between sexual love and other forms of human love. There is an erotic element in all personal relationships—a fact that is neither unhealthy nor surprising, because sexual love in its full form is a particularization and intensification, called for by our limited concrete individuality, of a desire for sharing and unity that in principle includes all men.

Further, sexual love for some people, however one wishes to account for the fact, is realized homosexually with a person of the same sex rather than heterosexually with a person of the opposite sex. Again, there are various degrees of sexual love in its specific form. People have generally to go through a period of trying to discover whether the mutual attraction is strong enough for a deep sexual relationship. There may even be a number of false starts with different people before a genuine relationship is established.

All this diversity in the concrete realization of sexual love raises the question of the appropriate expression of sexual love in its different manifestations and degrees. Sex in its narrowest meaning refers to genital intercourse and to the mutual exchanges immediately connected with such intercourse. Among religious people, most discussions of sex are still chiefly concerned with whether the traditional rule, limiting genital expression to a lifelong monogamous marriage is to be upheld. I, personally, do not regard that as the main issue, which for me is the opposition between two fundamentally different modes of sexual activity; namely, the sensuous and the sensual. But to avoid any impression of evasiveness, I must first, before discussing that, give some direct answers to the common questions.

Every sexual expression takes place within a particular cultural setting and takes its weight of meaning from that setting. To hug and kiss someone in one culture has a different meaning, is consequently a different human action, and implies a different feeling response than in another culture. That does not mean that one's culture cannot be criticized or that it is not open to change. For example, in my opinion, English and American culture, at least in its Anglo-Saxon variety, unduly inhibits gestures of warm affection between men because of a fear of homosexuality. Again, this whole book is a small attempt to move our present culture in a given direction. But the cultural mediation of all sexual expression does mean that one can never act as though in a cultural vacuum. Because premarital intercourse is a light matter in some primitive cultures, it does not follow that it can be treated as trivial in a Western country, even if one decides that it is sometimes appropriate. Decisions of conduct have to be made with reference to people as they actually are in concrete circumstances of time and place.

Further, since sexual activity affects the social order, society inevitably has some measure of interest in it, and in fact every society has laws and institutions affecting sexual conduct. Modern urban societies are functionally less integrated than previous societies; and so, unlike earlier functionally close-knit societies, a wide variety of sexual customs can and do exist in them without interfering with other areas of societal life. That is even more so now when the link between sex and children is a matter of choice. All the same, even in modern societies, there are social norms and institutions governing sexual behavior. We all internalize the laws and institutions of our society, at least to some degree, so that they determine as well as mediate our feeling responses. Sexual love, unconditioned culturally and untrammeled by institutions, is not a reality but a creation of fantasy.

Nevertheless, there is always some lack of fit between human spontaneity of feelings and their externalization in laws, institutions, and customs. The literature of the world is full of examples of sexual love clashing with the established order governing its expression. It is simply untrue to see all such instances of uninstitutionalized love as a sinful giving way to an unruly sensual passion. On the contrary, they are often a true liberation of the human spirit over law. Sensuality more frequently establishes the institution of brothels than it allows itself to fall inopportunely into love.

What all this comes to is that, while I consider "free love" or "natural sex" without laws or institutions immature fantasies, I do not regard any of the laws, institutions, and customs regulating sexual activity as absolute. Moreover, I can easily conceive of instances in our present culture—which, in any event, is in a period of change and experimentation in regard to its sexual customs and institutions—when premarital or extramarital genital intercourse is good and appropriate. The traditional Christian rule is culturally relative and open to exceptions and to change.

Genital intercourse, like all other human physical actions, is capable of bearing differing weights of meaning. It certainly varies in meaning within marriage itself. There is no convincing proof that it should always have the meaning of a lasting and fully attained sexual love and sharing of lives. It may be exploratory rather than an expression of an achieved union. Even where it does express the full emergence of sexual love, it may at times be appropriate, indeed even morally demanded, that the consummation precede the official marriage. To give a literary example of that: In Morley Callaghan's novel,

The Loved and the Lost, Jim McAlpine does wrong and fails in love as a human being by not sleeping with Peggy Sanderson on the night she wants and needs him.[15] Likewise, in regard to extramarital intercourse, marriage and sexual love do not always coincide and sometimes it is better not to insist upon making them do so; also, one cannot absolutely exclude genital intercourse as the expression in some circumstances of a secondary relationship.

Needless to say, the traditional rule does indeed enshrine a wisdom which it would be silly to ignore. If genital intercourse is used too freely for lesser manifestations of sexual love, it may well lose its power to express that love at a deeper level. Just as words can be degraded and lose their expressiveness and firmness of meaning by careless and excessive use, so can symbolic actions like sexual intercourse. Much subtlety and power of expression has been lost by the sexual garrulity of our society in word and action, and by its childish desire to develop personal relationships at the speed of jet flight. A delicate restraint of expression in sex, as in speech, is not identical with inhibition, but may come from the wish to say more and say it more effectively.

Again, the unity of hearts and lives desired by sexual love is usually achieved in the present disordered situation of humanity only through painful struggle. The virtues of fidelity and patience are needed to reach the higher levels of union. If partners break off their union at the first difficult patch, they are likely to spend their lives in a frustrated search for a kind of love they are, in effect, refusing before they even start on each new sexual relationship.

But I do not wish to continue this casuistry of sexual problems. Much of the difficulty in making practical decisions comes from the supposition that sex is a massive, primordial force, a bodily energy that is the source of barely controllable impulses, so that to keep it from

engulfing human existence it has to be held back by laws
and institutions made irrationally absolute as taboos. To
admit an exception to a law or suggest a change in an
institution might, it is feared, weaken and perhaps destroy the dam that confines the flood of sexual desires. I
reject that assumption as false and see no reason why
questions of sexual conduct should be treated with such
fevered fear.

What I have already said about the body applies fully
to sexuality. Sexuality may be lived as sensuousness or as
sensuality; and the roots of sensuality lie in the mind, not
in the body. Sex is sensuousness when we participate in
the spontaneous sexual rhythms and responses of the
body and are open to the joys and delights, the pain,
suffering, and stress of sexual experience. As sensuous,
we allow the spontaneous sexual responsiveness of the
body to hold sway and suspend the controlling and driving impetus of the rational mind and will.

True, in the present condition of humanity, a first
innocence in the sexual sphere is as unavailable as in
other areas of human experience. We have to struggle
through to a second innocence. But we do so, neither by
fearing the body as sexual nor by a punitive discipline. To
seek a complete rational control over sexual responses is
a false ideal. We have to trust the body and endeavor to
retrieve its spontaneous rhythms. The discipline of
achieved spontaneity is as appropriate here as elsewhere.
Although there is much chaff among the wheat, many
books of popular psychology concerning the growth of
personal relationships and the role of sex are far health-
ier and more useful than most books of traditional
spiritual guidance on sex.

Sexual spontaneity is culturally conditioned and institutionally mediated, though it is frequently found in a
dialectical tension with current mores and institutions.
Decisions concerning the fostering and expression of
particular sexual responses will be by a comparative ap-

prehension of the perhaps conflicting values in the concrete situation. Sex as sensuality is the submission of the sexual faculty to the driving, straining consciousness of a mind alienated from its bodiliness. It is deprived both of its meaning as a relationship of personal love and of its mystical associations; the body both of oneself and of the other is reduced to a physical object to be used instrumentally for purposes—pleasure, power, reassurance, and so forth—of the egocentric self.

The supposed uncontrollable sexual urges of the body are in fact the reflection of the compulsive drives of an empty, isolated, threatened ego, trying to fill up its emptiness or protect its unstable, unreal self and world against the shattering impact of genuine feeling. What are called sexual problems are problems of the total personality.

Sex, then, in its outward form is, like death, an ambiguous symbol. When genuine, sex is a privileged expression of love. Love is living with reality: self-love with the reality of ourselves, altruistic love with the reality of others, love of God with total reality. And feeling is the way we embrace reality with our real, undivided selves. Sexual love is a feeling response that puts us in touch with the reality of ourselves as bodily persons, opens us to intimate union with the reality of another person—and indirectly to the reality of other people—and takes us up into a movement of self-transcendence that leads to God.

But sex can also be a horrifying image of sin, understood as the misuse of human higher potentialities to block their open dynamism and twist them back to serve the purposes of an enclosed, egocentric self. In Joseph Heller's novel, *Something Happened,*[16] Bob Slocum's sensual pursuit of sex mirrors the meaninglessness of his empty life, incapacitated as he is by modern life for joy or genuine love. Again, what better picture of hell is there than a loveless marriage, in which two people slowly destroy each other in defending their enclosed selves?

The phrase "living in sin" applies much more accurately to such a marriage than to a love relationship outside marriage. Sensuality is sinful, not because it is an indulgence in unlawful pleasure, but because of the loveless self-centeredness it expresses. What is morally repellent in the "girlie" magazines is not the photos of nudes—which though often vulgar are sometimes delightful—but the accompanying text and articles, which with their debased values truly degrade the human spirit.

Sex in its genuine form as sensuous love is sacramental in its power to move persons out of self-centeredness into an openness in which they meet God. Does this leave any place for celibacy as a religious vocation? One must first frankly say that celibacy as it has been lived and motivated in Christian history has more often than not been an impairment of the human spirit. It has rarely been free of negative attitudes toward the body, and in particular toward sexuality; and it has also been entangled in the power games of the Church as an institution. Nevertheless, it is possible to conceive of it as a genuine call, though a rare one.

The movement of the human person toward transcendent values is usually mediated through the various phases of an unfolding human life, including the finding and development of an intimate relationship of sexual love. But a person can be so overtaken by a mystical sense of the transcendent, by a dedication to the needs of some fellow human beings, or by some cause, that he or she is existentially disabled in regard to forming an intimate relationship with another individual person.[17] Celibacy is thus an ecstatic disengagement from the ordinary course of human relationships, which in no way implies any negative attitude to them. For it not to result in an injurious stunting of the person and an enclosure upon the self, the ecstatic pull out of the self that causes it must be powerful enough to offset the loss of the self-transcending effect of a shared life of intimate love with another person. Moreover, of its nature, celibacy will often be a temporary call, the result of a mystical absorption or altruistic dedication lasting for a limited period.

All the same, once every negative attitude to the body has been eliminated, by far the commonest path to mystical union and self-transcending dedication is sexual love when genuinely sensuous and not sensual, so that sexual love and transcendent love can find a single expression, as in this Bengali lyric:

> When my beloved returns to my house
> I shall make my body the altar of joy
> and let down my hair to sweep it.
> My twisting necklace of pearls shall be the intricate,
> sprinkled design on the altar,
> my full breasts the water jars,
> my curved hips the plantain trees,
> the tinkling bells at my waist the young shoots of the
> mango.
> I shall use the arcane arts of fair women in all lands
> to make my beauty outshine a thousand moons.[18]

VII.
Toward a Critique
of Religious Experience

The dominance in present culture of abstract reason, with the consequent dichotomy between rationality and affectivity, makes suspect any account of religion that stresses the primacy of feeling. People suppose that what is being advocated is a return to a precritical attitude, surrendering the gains of modern critical intelligence, which has liberated society and the individual from authoritatively imposed beliefs and practices not open to rational questioning.

On the other hand, those who recognize that the preceding analysis of religious feeling has in fact subjected elements of the historical Christian tradition to criticism will want to ask about the criteria used and the standpoint from which the critique has been made. From both these points of view, it seems necessary to conclude this book on religious feeling with a statement of the meaning and function of criticism in relation to religious experience.

To avoid confusion, it should be noted at the outset that criticism or critical reflection is a second-order activity that presupposes and does not create the first-order activity upon which it reflects. The critique of religious experience is reflection upon religious experience; it presupposes religion as a datum transmitted through the processes proper to religious traditions. It is not its function to construct a religion but to reflect upon religion as it is found. Religious feeling is first and fundamentally given and transmitted prereflectively, bodily, symbolically, and in action. It does not wait upon criticism in that process. At the same time, the prereflective gives rise to reflection and demands to be thematized and justified at the critical level. And critical reflection can and does have repercussions upon first-order religious experience, leading to salutary revisions and corrections.

But what is criticism? The question must first be answered in general terms and then the answer applied to the criticism of religious experience. Criticism may be defined as a process of self-reflection motivated by an interest in emancipation. It is a reflection that uncovers and appropriates the freedom and creative autonomy of the self in its world.

Through reflection the self becomes aware of the formative processes which create every society and every individual. It consciously grasps the prior conditions of every region of experience, with its objects, actions, and interests. The uncovering of those conditions manifests where and how each type of experience is grounded and allows an explicit determination of its limits and validity.

Such reflection is emancipatory because it dissolves the apparent necessity of the given world and reveals the creative potentiality of men for freely constructing their world and themselves or, better, their selves in their world.

There is a contrast here between a mythical and a critical consciousness. A mythical consciousness accepts an order of the world and society as given prior to man's freedom and imposing itself upon him as necessary; whereas for a critical consciousness, society and the world are products of human freedom, remaining subject to the creative power that constructed them. Again, for a mythical consciousness there is an unquestionable order; for a critical consciousness everything is under questioning. Criticism is universal in principle; to limit it is essentially to destroy it.

The use of "criticism" and "critical" in the sense described is taken from Kant. Kant did not fully recognize the historical dimension of critical reflection and, as a consequence, he gave the categories his criticism uncovered an uncritical necessity. Nevertheless, his critical philosophy, taken as a whole, was emancipatory in intent and effect. It should be interpreted in relation with his writings on history; for example, in the essay, "What is Enlightenment?" he speaks of the overcoming of man's self-incurred tutelage.[1]

Besides its dissolution of a mythical consciousness, critical reflection is emancipatory in two further ways, corresponding to two tasks explicitly formulated since Kant. The first is the psychoanalytic task of uncovering the structures of repression in the individual. These structures block the freedom of the individual and inhibit his creativity. They put him in bondage to unconscious drives and systematically distort his personal actions, their expression and their products. Whatever the hesitations about the particular concepts, hypotheses, and theories of Freud, no critical consciousness can now ignore his contribution or evade the task his work drew attention to. That is why the Germans include Freud among the representative thinkers of the *Aufklärung*. Critical reflection upon any region of human experience has now to ask how far a genetic explanation shows its form and contents to be the product of neurotic repression rather than of uninhibited creativity and freedom.

Not that we can dismiss the products of neurosis as valueless, but such an origin is relevant to their critical evaluation.

Critical reflection is emancipatory in a second way, in being a critique of ideologies. Ideology is a distortion resulting from social structures of domination and violence, analogous to the structures of repression in the individual as uncovered by Freudian psychoanalysis. The critique of ideologies on the social and political level carries out the functions performed by psychoanalysis on the individual level. In other words, just as on the individual level a critical consciousness demands that we enquire how far stances, responses, assertions, and decisions are distorted by the blind spots and inhibitions resulting from repression, so also on the social level criticism requires us to uncover the hidden, systematic distortions produced by repressive social structures. A process of simple interpretation is not enough when dealing with the products of social consciousness. Critical reflection must also develop genetic explanations to account for the ideologies that trammel social communication.

Both psychoanalysis and the critique of ideologies can be seen as parts of total process directed toward the achievement of unimpeded communication. Psychoanalysis is concerned with internal communication within the subject, communication between the organic and psychic, namely, the unconscious and consciousness, so that the two levels work in harmony with a free flow between them. The critique of ideologies in its turn aims at a liberation that would establish a communication free from domination, unconstrained and non-manipulative, within society among its various groups.

In brief, criticism is reflection that brings to consciousness the formative processes behind the individual and society. It thus enables men to appropriate their creative freedom and liberate themselves from the repression and domination that distort their self-formation.

A problem that thinkers have struggled with since the emergence of critical reflection is its relationship with tradition. Historically, it was a question of overcoming the limitations and one-sidedness of the Enlightenment of the *philosophes*. Here it must be enough to summarize conclusions. Human freedom is not the freedom of atomic individuals or windowless monads, but the freedom of men in community. The individual is not an absolute subject, with other men related to him only as objects of his thoughts or actions. The subject of human thought and action is a social group, a "we." Not that we should reify the social group as an entity existing apart from the individuals composing it, but the individual acts only within and from out of a network of social relationships. That network, with the interactions it includes and the institutions it creates, is not reducible to any of the individuals it comprises.

Again, human creative autonomy is that proper to an historical subject acting within history. Creation by men is not creation *ex nihilo* by ahistorical subjects. Both these considerations converge to show that a primordial relation of participation binds men to traditions that precede them. Since our being is social and historical, we begin within a received culture transmitted as a tradition, and the fundamental way we remain related to the social-historical is by belonging. There is no transcendent, neutral point of view from which we can survey the mess of traditions corrupted by repression and ideology. There is no absolute reason, stripped of all prejudgments, allowing us to engage in a critical reflection that would dominate the cultural materials through purely objective techniques.

This should not mean, however, that critical reflection should be excluded and that we should swing back to a precritical approach. The traditions we receive as our cultural heritage are not just places of truth and freedom, but places of untruth and unfreedom. Hence, there must be a moment of critical distance and an element of discriminating reflection.

At the same time, the recognition that there is no absolute starting point distinguishes dialectical criticism from the abstract critical reason of rationalism and empiricism. Both rationalism and empiricism, though each in its own way, seek to establish some absolutely certain ground on which everything else can be based. Rationalism claims to confine it in a set (containing perhaps only one) of necessary, self-evident truths, serving as principles from which all else can be deduced. Empiricism appeals to events observable by the senses and recorded in protocol statements. On the basis of these, scientific laws are established and scientific hypotheses verified.

The rationalist and empiricist viewpoints, though developing methods of real though limited value, are abstract because they omit consideration of the historical, social, cultural context that conditions all human knowing. Neither reasoning nor observation are ahistorical and unaffected by the social and historical situation of the reasoner or observer.

Thus, freedom can easily become an empty concept, so fluid that it is devoid of consistency or content. To be given a meaning, it must be connected with traditions having an interest in freedom, the traditions from which the ideal and concept originally emerged. Again, criticism can become an empty negativity, an exercise in missing the point. To be meaningfully criticized, elements (particular truths or "facts") must be related to the whole of which they are parts, and which alone give them meaning. That whole is a tradition as a coherent unity.

There are two possibilities. The elements may be criticized from a position of belonging to the tradition of which they are a part. There is then a movement from the tradition to the criticism of its elements and back to the tradition as reinterpreted and reappropriated. Or the elements may be criticized from outside the tradition of which they are parts. In that case, they must still be considered in the context of the whole to which they belong; but the critic has the further task of bringing his own tradition or total view into relation with the tradition the elements of which he is criticizing.

Criticism, therefore, involves a continuous movement to and fro, from parts to whole and from whole to parts. Critical discourse oscillates between particular truths and facts and overall syntheses, between the totality of a constructed world and its particular elements. Because criticism as dialectical refuses the project of finding an absolute starting point analytically in particular truths or facts, and insists upon an unceasing movement from elements of thought and action to their concrete historical context and back, it has the discernment of coherent wholes in the flux of history as a basic task.

What constitutes a coherent whole in the context of which particular elements of thought and action may be understood, criticized, and evaluated? A tradition and the social group that carries it; or, in an equivalent formulation, a social group with its tradition. Tradition here means more than an intellectual scheme. Philosophies and theologies are abstract; they are not concrete wholes, and therefore they are not of themselves fully intelligible. A tradition is a way of responding to reality, including feelings, memories, images, ideas, theories, forms of language, modes of action, aspirations, ideals, attitudes, interpersonal relationships: in brief, the entire complex that constitutes life within a particular world, a world bounded by an horizon that determines the particular sense of reality that pervades it.

A tradition in that concrete sense is correlative to a social group and cannot be adequately considered apart from the social group which carries it. Tradition and social group determine each other. What unites a social group and distinguishes it from other groups is the tradition it bears. What constitutes a tradition is the way of life, the consciousness and praxis, of a social group. But clearly not all social groupings are coherent wholes deserving consideration of themselves, not simply as elements of a wider whole; and not all forms of thought and action have sufficient range to be traditions in the sense used. Hence, the fundamental critical task of discerning the significant dividing lines among social groups and their traditions. This discernment is itself subject to modification in the dialectical process.

On the basis of a discernment of coherent wholes, criticism proceeds by uncovering the formative processes that created them, together with the inhibitions and oppressions that, in their regard, obstructed the working of human creativity and freedom. Then, in the light of that critique, it discusses the validity of those totalities and their limits.

To turn now to the critical enterprise as applied to religious experience, understood in the comprehensive sense as including all the activities and passivities we call religious. The critique of religious experience has to identify and discuss that experience as embodied and expressed. The approach, therefore, must be through religious language, if language is taken in the widest sense as the articulation of experience in expressive forms.

The language of religion does not primarily consist of doctrinal statements, even less of the assertions of speculative theology. The primary language of religion is found "embedded in such modes of discourse as narratives, prophecies, legislative texts, proverbs, and wisdom sayings, hymns, prayers, and liturgical formulas."[2] To these strictly linguistic forms should be added the forms of action, aesthetic and practical, which also enter into first-order religious expression.

Critical reflection upon religion, therefore, presupposes a poetics of religious expression. The task of such a poetics is to identify and classify the various literary and artistic forms used to articulate religious experience. The meaning of religious expression is determined by the various modes of articulation proper to each literary or artistic form. To discuss the meaning of religious language in general is too vague and crude to be fruitful; and to avoid this, religious language should not be restricted, as by some analysts, to doctrinal and religio-metaphysical statements. In short, critical reflection upon the meaning and truth of religion simply cannot bypass the preliminary work of a poetics of religion.

The use of the word "poetics" already reflects a critical choice. It corresponds to the conviction that religious forms, linguistic and other, are the products of the creative imagination. By the creative imagination I refer, not simply to the picturing faculty, but, more importantly, to the constructive, poetic intelligence. "Poetic," because religious images, concepts, and words are not the direct formulation of observational or introspective data. They do not express directly known objects. They are the indirect and metaphorical evocation and articulation of a transcendent intentionality or dynamic in human experience. God is not a known object but a poetic idea. To suppose otherwise is idolatry. This is not to dismiss religious language as emotive and not cognitive, but it is to place its mode of cognition in feeling, and thus nearer poetry than empirical science.

Values are apprehended by feelings, and feelings, as we have seen, are not mere emotions or bodily movements; they are responses that are total insofar as they come from the unity of the self as an embodied person or personal body. Feelings, I repeat, are bodily responses that are animated by intelligence and spiritual affectivity; or, conversely, embodied intelligent and affective responses. Religious feelings are the spontaneous, connatural responses to total reality as total. They are the arousal of our personal being—our intelligent and bodily, spiritual and material selves—by that total reality as variously mediated and articulated in the forms of religious reality.

Consequently, a critical approach to religious forms that simply interprets or comments intellectually upon its cognitive meaning is inadequate. We have to show how those forms relate to our sensibility. The critic must not dissolve them through commentary, supposing that only their meaning, as reformulated in his interpretation, is relevant, and not their impact. The critic must, instead, let them be, showing what they are and facilitating their action upon our feelings. To borrow Susan Sontag's term, we need an erotics of religion. We can apply here what she says of literary and art criticism: "The function of criticism should be to show *how it is what it is,* even that *it is what it is,* rather than to show *what it means.* In place of hermeneutics we need an erotics of art."[3]

A poetics of religion and an erotics of religion come together as a critical aesthetics of religion. Such a critical aesthetics should be the first stage in any criticism of religious experience and the presupposition for subsequent critical reflection upon religion.

In passing it may be noted that the demand for a critical aesthetics of religion is not in any conflict with insistence upon the social and political character of religion, such as is found, say, in the political theology of Metz. One must simply point to the discussion of aesthetics among Marxists and, in particular, to the great importance given to aesthetic theory and criticism in writers of the Frankfurt School of critical sociology, notably Adorno, Horkheimer, Benjamin, and Lowenthal.[4] Also worth mentioning is the thesis of Herbert Marcuse concerning the "new sensibility" as a political factor.[5] Metz himself has noted the task of developing a new critical aesthetics,[6] and the point has been taken up by one of the critics of his political theology.[7]

The work of critical aesthetics, in making clear the nature and functioning of the forms of religious expres-

sion in all their variety, leads to and overlaps with a
critical reflection upon the creative process through
which they emerge and articulate religious experience.
Further, the attempt to lay bare the formation of religion
and its prior conditions confronts critical reflection with
the question of structures of repression that may have
inhibited human creative freedom in that area of experience and distorted the process and its products.

Indeed, as is well known, Freud maintained that religion as a whole was a general neurosis, in the sense that
the mental processes and kinds of behavior involved in
religion were the same as those associated with neuroses.
Freud's contentions are not so easily dismissed as is sometimes thought.[8] But even were we to leave them aside, we
should still have to face the more moderate but widespread conviction of a conflict between traditional religion and the creative autonomy of modern men in relation to the world and society. There is, for example, the
deeply disturbing thesis formulated admirably by William Lynch in *Christ and Prometheus.*[9] Lynch argues that
the religious imagination in its older form has, in fact,
hindered the emergence of the secular in its autonomy.
Traditional religious images stress the conditionality of
the world; that is, they relate everything to a center, a
principle or condition outside itself, which alone gives it
meaning. Such images have blocked the secular project,
which he describes as "the march of mankind, in the
autonomous light of its own resources, toward the mas-
tery and humanization of the world."[10] The older religious image of the world "could not tolerate the basic
secular notion of *constitutive* autonomy and uncondi-
tional self-contained novelty."[11] It has imposed "its own
forms upon the world as final meaning,"[12] and in some
instances devalued the secular with negative images.
Consequently, in the present crisis of religion there has to
be vast desymbolizing processes, which will be a "descent
into hell" of the religious imagination, as it strips itself of
its older images.[13] Then one must struggle for a new

image of man and of his secular project. The question, therefore, arises: whether, for critical reflection, there is not an incompatibility between all traditional forms of the Christian tradition, together with most Christian theologies, and the modern process of emancipation with its stress upon human creative freedom. Does not the modern history of freedom, in which critical consciousness emerged and to which it belongs, mark a shift in human society and culture that has rendered traditional forms of religion obsolete?

John Wren-Lewis makes a distinction between two cultures or ways of responding to life: the traditional and the humanist-experimental. The traditional, represented by most religions but also by dogmatic materialism, is governed by the supreme need to reach some truly authoritative understanding of the realities behind common experience. The assumption is that there is an order, a grand design, beyond the realities of everyday experience. The concern is to discern and contemplate it; and then one's duty and purpose in life is to conform to it. For the modern, humanist, and experimental outlook "the world is *simply what we know it to be in the practical business of meeting it, handling it and doing things in it*—not so much a thing—a system, a reality, an order—as an opportunity, a potentiality for creative action."[14]

One is reminded here of Marx's view of the relation between theory and praxis.[15] Marx rejected the notion of theory independent of praxis, theory as a presuppositionless, contemplative recognition of a stable object. Praxis, ranging from bodily labor and production to political revolution, was the only source of meaning. Theory was the consciousness of praxis; and so, theoretical activity, like the practical activity with which it is one, is a product of the changing reality of society and of the relationship with nature mediated by society. That was the context for Marx's rejection of religion. What characterized thought as religious for Marx was its being mere theory divorced from social practice. By claiming permanent and universal truth in theory as if it were independent of social conditions, religion uncritically reflected patterns of social dominance and concealed social reality in mystifying abstractions. Religion and theology claimed a purely theoretical center of reference for their truth and its continuing identity.

For John Wren-Lewis, traditional religion is a way of avoiding the challenges and responsibilities of human creativity and freedom; and, following Freud, he sees the steady decline of the traditional outlook as "a gradual escape from the bondage of an age-long state of neurotic inhibition."[16] For Marx, religion was ideology through and through, a denial of concrete history, an escape into abstraction and a mystification of social dominance.

I refer once more to what will be regarded by some as all too familiar negative critiques of religion, not to parade them for acceptance, but to make it obvious that a critique of religion focused upon the verifiability or falsifiability of doctrinal statements, or concerned with the validity of proofs for the existence of God and with similar matters, is largely missing the point. Criticism, understood as reflection motivated by an interest in emancipation, is concerned with religious traditions as concrete, coherent wholes. It is an attempt to uncover and bring to awareness the formative processes, both individual and social, which have created and articulated a particular tradition. Its interest in human creative freedom, and in unconstrained social communication without domination, will make it sensitive to the distortions due to neurotic inhibition and social oppression. It cannot be content with intellectual discussions *in vacuo*.

Doctrinal or theological statements cannot be interpreted outside a context. Just as words need the context of the sentence to give them a determinate meaning, and as sentences need the context of a particular work composed according to a literary genre and in an individual style to give them their meaning, so also particular works have to be interpreted in the context of a total coherent whole; namely, a tradition and the social group that carries it. To attempt to analyze and evaluate religious statements outside of their total context is to fall into the abstract thinking of empiricism or rationalism, and the myth of some absolute starting point. A dialectical critique of religion will pass from an examination of individual statements to the investigation of the whole of which they are elements, and then back from a grasp of the whole to a further interpretation and assessment of the individual statements. The concrete coherent whole to be discerned by the critique of religion in its dialectical method will be a distinct religious tradition as correlative to a social group.

"Religious tradition" has taken on a narrowly intellectual meaning as an inherited set of beliefs. That is not the meaning intended here. I am using it to include praxis as well as theory. In short, as previously stated, a tradition embraces the entire complex that constitutes life within a particular world; it is a way, comprehensively considered, of responding to reality.

The term "religious tradition" may also mislead by creating the supposition that the discrimination of religious traditions is already an accomplished fact in the rough-and-ready division of the world religions or, in the Christian context, in the association of each tradition with a particular Church. That supposition is far from being the case in fact. The discrimination of different traditions is a delicate task, requiring much detailed work. An illustration of this is Lucien Goldmann's careful reconstruction of the tragic vision as a total world view or vision of reality, found as such in Pascal and Racine. Goldmann's book, I may remark, is methodologically most stimulating and I have been much helped by it.[17] It also makes clear that a religious tradition as distinctive cannot be identified with adherence to a particular

Church. Descartes and Malebranche on the one hand, and Pascal and Racine on the other, were Catholics, but they represented two very different religious traditions as ways of responding to reality. In any major Christian Church, especially over a period of time, there are several substantially different religions, even if those belonging to them all recite the same creeds.

A key task of the critique of religion, therefore, is to develop a typology of religious traditions. For the Christian religion, which is my present concern, we have histories of theology, but these set forth a series of similar intellectual schemata, inserted for the most part simply into the biographical context of their originators. Such accounts remain abstract and are of defective intelligibility. To put it bluntly, they do not make complete sense. Can there be a "history" of theology, other than a correlation of abstractions?

Within the Christian context, there are also some accounts of different ways of doing theology—typologies of theology.[18] But are not these again exercises in abstraction? Theologies are not pure, uncontaminated intellectual enterprises; they are influenced by a variety of interests. They are not self-contained entities; they are parts of a wider whole. They cannot be intelligently studied apart from other writings coming out of the same tradition taken as a whole. To make complete sense, they have to be replaced in the economic, social, political, literary, and artistic life of the social groups from which they sprang. No doubt, formal and logical studies of theological statements and systems are needed for conceptual clarification, but we should not suppose that such studies enable us to know what is going on when theologies are produced and clash. It is now well recognized that the Trinitarian and Christological controversies in the early Church do not make sense apart from the economic, social, and political struggles of which they were one form of expression. The difference between liberal and neo-orthodox theologies, or between

neo-Thomism and transcendental Thomism, is not confined to some realm of pure theological ideas. The difference, in the concrete, was one of social, political, and
religious praxis. Feminist theology in its turn has drawn
attention to the economic, social, and political infrastruc-
ture of theological images, concepts, statements, and
theories. Therefore, what is needed for critical reflection
is a discrimination of traditions as distinctive wholes, not
the listing, seriatim, or the classification of theological
schemata or procedures.

A tradition is correlative with the social group that
carries it. What are the social groups to which the different religious traditions belong? To determine these is
also the task of the critique of religion.

Working within an overall Christian context—which
is my own concrete starting point—we can take different
theologies as clues to different religious traditions, insofar as a theology is either a direct or, if neurotically or
ideologically distorted, an indirect abstract expression of
a concrete form of life. We can then ask which social
groups produced which theologies. For example, the
theology of Thomas Aquinas, together with Aristotelian
Scholastic theology in general, has been connected with
the growth of the cities and the emergence of the
medieval bourgeoisie.[19] To turn to the contemporary
situation, the theology of secularization has been seen as
the ideology of those Christians who socially and politi-
cally intend to conform to the values and praxis of advanced industrial society.[20] Clearly, such general statements must be made more precise and also supported by
detailed investigations. When that is done, the particular
theology itself must be merged into a greater whole with
other theoretical elements and with social and religious
praxis.

A complication of modern times is that theology has
increasingly become a form of expression reserved to
ecclesiastics. The clergy usually draws its members from
different social classes, but these members become to a

great extent *déclassés* and form a distinct social group. Consequently, the discernment of the social basis and functioning of an ecclesiastically produced theology is a question of determining the role and function of the Church at a particular time and place. Clerical theology is carried by the social group that serves the Church as a particular institution with a particular though varying function within society. Hence, its lack of appeal to the laity and their hostility to some manifestations of it.

Something similar must be said of academic theology, produced in the universities and more or less free from ecclesiastical control. The academic context has been particularly important in the development of German theology. Its social basis has to be determined by examining the role and functioning of the universities. In passing, the recent change being brought about in Catholic theology, by its move from the environment of the seminary to that of the university, might be noted. A different social group is beginning to develop its theology. Earlier there was the great influence of Blondel, whose religious thinking was done outside the strictly ecclesiastical orbit.

At the same time, if one considers, not the social groups serving the institutions of Church and university, but other social groups within modern society, it is apparent that theology for them has ceased to be the dominant expression of religious thought. Any critique of religious experience today that confines itself to theological writing is playing on the periphery. Even apart from its expression in action, religion today is articulated in other than theological writing; namely, philosophical, literary, political, and, indeed, scientific in the social sciences. For example, no adequate account of religion in the nineteenth and twentieth centuries is possible without a study of the novel.

To repeat, then: the critique of religion is concerned with religious traditions and the social groups which carry them. That does not mean with systems of theology and the theologians who produce them. Criticism as dialectical endeavors to discern and evaluate totalities; namely, the forms of life and consciousness of social groups.

But what are the criteria of evaluation once different religious traditions have been discerned? If one is convinced that theory and knowledge are subordinate to the wider and deeper movement of human existence as an integrated whole, then inevitably one will ask what are the interests in terms of which a particular form of human knowing is justified. Jürgen Habermas distinguished three kinds of interest as fundamental to three kinds of knowledge. First, the strict sciences yield information that presupposes the interest of certainty and technical control. Second, the hermeneutic sciences give an understanding of the social and cultural life-world that presupposes the interest of extending intersubjective communication. Third, there is a critical science, which is an inquiry capable of dissolving the apparent necessity of historical modes of authority, of creating an awareness of the self-formative processes of society and the self, and which has an interest in emancipation as its presupposition.[21] For me, the critique of religion, like criticism in general, is motivated by an interest in emancipation. It will, therefore, evaluate religious traditions by the criterion of their relation to human emancipation.

However, I should want to interpret emancipation in a fashion similar to Metz's development of the concept of freedom.[22] Human freedom is never simply the self-possession of man, but is always at the same time the opening of man to the transcendence of God. To achieve a religious understanding of freedom without losing touch with social and political realities is not easy. All the same, I should maintain that freedom, given a sufficiently profound grasp of freedom, can become the most important interest for men, the key value or criterion in assessing the truth and value of those concrete modes of life I have called religious traditions. It should be added that neither the understanding of freedom nor its use as a criterion can be achieved in theory alone, but only in and through feeling and praxis.

Any evaluation of religious traditions will also be partly comparative. In other words, a tradition has the greater claim to truth and value when it can integrate the positive elements of other traditions into itself as into a higher synthesis, while overcoming their insufficiencies and defects. The dialectical method, in insisting upon the consideration, not just of isolated elements, but of totalities, always seeks the greater totality as surpassing partial syntheses. Implicit in this comparative criterion is the criterion of adequacy to human experience. The claim to truth of any concrete form of life must be judged by the extent to which it does justice to all the data and exigencies of human experience.

That leaves us with the question of the standpoint of the critic; or, to put it in another way, the tradition to which he belongs and from which he engages in critical reflection. Historically speaking, there is no doubt that the concept of critical reflection I have been expounding and applying comes out of that movement for emancipation and enlightenment which has been a feature of the modern epoch in the West. It belongs to what Metz calls the modern history of freedom (*die neuzeitliche Freiheits-geschichte*);[23] or, alternatively, the *Aufklärungsproszesz* or *Aufklärungstradition*, understood as the attempt of a line of thinkers from Kant onwards to overcome the one-sidedness of the abstract reason of the Enlightenment in its first phase, with its rationalism and empiricism, without returning to an uncritical acceptance of tradition or of authoritarian Christianity.[24]

When, however, Christians like myself take our stand within that tradition and engage in a critical reflection that rejects rationalism and empiricism on the one hand, and any final appeal to external authority on the other, are we still within the Christian tradition? Is there a Christian form of the critical tradition? Or is it not more honest to say that insights from the Christian tradition have been integrated with other insights into a higher synthesis, no longer in any authentic sense Christian?

Historically and sociologically, it is difficult to place the modern thrust toward freedom and creative autonomy through emancipatory praxis and critical consciousness within the Christian tradition. Almost every step in the emergence of modern freedom and criticism has been opposed by most representatives of the Christian tradition. Further, traditional Christian imagery is in conflict with modern autonomy, as we have seen in Lynch's call for a vast desymbolization. Moreover, the idea of a once-for-all revelation and final truth, which would seem to be at the heart of the Christian vision of the world and the Christian mode of life, essentially contradicts the changing, experimental, constructive character of human truth for a free and critical consciousness. Truth for critical reflection, unlike the Christian conception, cannot be handed to us ready-made for our acceptance; it arises out of the struggle for liberation and is always proportionate to the actualization of our creative freedom.

On the other hand, in a recent essay Robert Morgan has argued most effectively that criticism, in the light of an apprehension of the Christian Gospel, has been a regular and characteristic feature of the ever-expanding Christian tradition:

> The proclamation of the Gospel requires the religious tradition, but it always and necessarily involves critical interpretation of that tradition. Normally where the tradition is functioning smoothly as a vehicle of the Christian revelation this critical interpretation will be a matter of selection and emphasis. But where the tradition is choking or strangling the expression of this liberating Gospel, then proclamation must involve attacking the tradition. In these cases critical interpretation of the tradition is radicalized.[25]

Further, there is the complicated question of the emigration of Christian values out of the Christian Churches into what, particularly since the Enlightenment, has become the much wider area of Western culture. How far do the official representatives of the Christian tradition in the institutional sense still represent the Christian tradition in its authentic line of development?

Both the existence of a constant critical voice within the Christian tradition and the widespread presence in modern times of Christian values outside the Churches make one hesitate to regard the modern critical enterprise as not belonging to the Christian tradition, at least to some degree.

Such hesitation is increased by the fact that the tradition of emancipation and criticism is itself in jeopardy today. The difficulty of identifying which social groups now carry it points up the problem of its survival in modern technocratic society. Perhaps the scattered bands of those who still give it their allegiance may, in their creative reinterpretation and reappropriation of it in the difficult contemporary situation, find themselves drawing upon further resources of the Christian tradition. In which case a deeper affinity than previously suspected between the modern critical and the Christian traditions may be uncovered. It must be remembered that criticism as a second-order activity depends upon the prereflective, symbolic transmission of values at the first-order level. The Christian symbolic inheritance is so rich and so deeply embedded in Western culture that, whatever modifications and enrichments it may receive from other traditions, it is still the inevitable starting point for those in the West concerned with transcendent values.

Nevertheless, critical reflection has to come to grips with the concrete reality of an existing tradition, not just with the programmatic ideal of some writer. To suppose otherwise is to turn criticism into ideology. Consequently, it has to be said frankly that the critique of religion is at present in conflict with most existing forms of the Christian tradition as organized institutionally. It is as yet unclear whether any of these forms have the potentiality of developing in such a way as to integrate the values of modern criticism into itself. Or, to put it as Robert Morgan does: "A central question for Christianity today is whether its radicals and conservatives finally part company."[26]

Notes

Notes to Chapter I
FEELING AS THE HUMAN
RESPONSE TO REALITY

1. T. S. Eliot, "Burnt Norton," *Collected Poems 1909-1962* (London: Faber and Faber, 1963), p. 190.

2. Erich Fromm, *The Art of Loving* (New York: Bantam Books, 1963), p. 101.

3. Arthur Janov, *The Primal Scream: Primal Therapy, the Cure for Neurosis* (New York: Delta, 1970), p. 68.

4. "Certain Noble Plays of Japan" in *Essays and Introductions* (London: Macmillan, 1961), p. 235.

5. "Three Myths of Transcendence" in *Transcendence,* ed. Herbert W. Richardson and Donald R. Cutler (Boston: Beacon Press, 1969), p. 99.

6. Wilfred Cantwell Smith, *The Meaning and the End of Religion: A New Approach to the Religious Traditions of Mankind.* A Mentor Book (New York: New American Library, 1964).

7. Max Weber, *The Sociology of Religion* (London: Methuen, 1965), ch. 12: "Soteriology and Types of Salvation," pp. 184-206.

8. For a discussion of this distinction, see Charles Davis, *Christ and the World Religions* (London: Hodder & Stoughton/New York: Herder & Herder, 1970), pp. 118-24.

9. Ninian Smart, *Philosophers and Religious Truth,* 2nd ed. (London: SCM Press, 1969), p. 115.

10. Fontana ed.; (London: Collins, 1960), p. 47.

11. *Ibid.*, pp. 47-8.

12. In *Truth and Dialogue: The Relationship Between World Religions,* ed. John Hick. (London: Sheldon Press, 1974), p. 55.

13. Ninian Smart, *The Yogi and the Devotee: The Interplay Between the Upanishads and Catholic Theology* (London: Allen & Unwin, 1968), pp. 66-74.

14. *Philosophers and Religious Truth,* p. 116.

15. Chapter 6. I have used the edition of Justin McCann, Golden Library Edition (London: Burns & Oates, 1964).

Notes to Chapter II
THE RELIGIOUS REFUSAL
OF THE BODY

1. From "About Disinterest." Cf. *Meister Eckhart: A Modern Translation* by Raymond Bernard Blakney, Harper Torchbooks (New York: Harper & Row, 1941), p. 90.

2. From "Ascent of Mount Carmel," chapter 4 Cf. *The Complete Works of Saint John of the Cross, Doctor of the Church,* trans. and ed. E. Allison Peers rev. ed. (London: Burns and Oates, 1953), vol. I, pp. 23-4.

3. *Ibid.*, p. 58.

4. Frederick Franck, *The Zen of Seeing, seeing/drawing as Meditation,* Vintage Books (New York: Random House, 1973), pp. 65-79.

5. Wallace Stevens, "Notes Toward a Supreme Fiction" in *The Collected Poems of Wallace Stevens* (London: Faber and Faber, 1945), p. 396.

6. (*Collected Poems,* pp. 52-3). The delightful short poem of Wallace Stevens, "The Apostrophe to Vincentine," from which the quoted phrase and other words are taken. The poet first figures Vincentine as nude, which made her seem monotonous, nameless earth. He then saw her as dressed and then as walking in a group and talking, a process which was the emergence of her as a full heavenly person.

7. John Wren-Lewis, *What Shall We Tell the Children?* (London: Constable, 1971), p. 152. Italics in the original. The outline of this chapter and the notes for it were finished before I came across Wren-Lewis's book. However, I found his book most useful in preparing my final text, although our views are not identical.

8. William James, *The Varieties of Religious Experience,* The Fontana Library (London: Collins, 1960), pp. 92-171.

9. *Ibid.,* p. 140.

10. *What Shall We Tell the Children?,* p. 130 (Italics in the original).

11. *Ibid.,* p. 156 (Italics in the original).

12. C. S. Lewis, *A Preface to Paradise Lost,* Oxford Paperbacks (London: Oxford University Press, 1960), chapter 10: "Milton and St. Augustine," pp. 66-72.

13. St. Augustine, *The City of God,* Everyman's Library (1945), vol. 2, p. 57.

14. *Ibid.,* p. 57.

15. *Ibid.,* p. 47.

16. *Ibid.,* p. 57.

17. *Ibid.,* p. 47.

18. Martin Turnell, *The Novel in France,* Peregrine Books (Harmondsworth: Penguin, 1962), pp. 70-1.

19. Morley Callaghan, *They Shall Inherit the Earth,* New Canadian Library (Toronto: McClelland and Stewart, 1969), p. 242.

20. For an account and assessment by a theologian of what he calls "the encounter-sensitivity-sensory awareness—Oriental meditation movement," see Harvey Cox, *The Seduction of the Spirit: The Use and Misuse of People's Religion* (New York: Simon and Schuster, 1973), chapter 8: "Naked Revival: Theology and the Human Potential Movement," pp. 197-225.

21. William Johnston, *Christian Zen* (New York: Harper & Row, 1971), p. 70. See also by the same author: *The Still Point: Reflections on Zen and Christian Mysticism* (New York: Fordham University Press, 1970); *Silent Music: The Science of Meditation* (New York, Harper & Row, 1974); and Thomas Merton, *Zen and the Birds of Appetite* (New York: New Directions, 1968).

22. *Ibid.,* p. 82.

23. *Ibid.*, pp. 3-4.

24. *Ibid.*, p. 4.

25. Eugen Herrigel, *Zen*, including *Zen in the Art of Archery* and *The Method of Zen*, McGraw-Hill Paperbacks (New York: McGraw-Hill, 1964).

26. From 'East Coker" in *Collected Poems 1909-1962* (London: Faber & Faber, 1963), p. 203.

Notes to Chapter III

FROM THE INTERIOR SELF
TO THE ISOLATED EGO

1. Eugen Herrigel, *Zen,* including *Zen in the Art of Archery* and *The Method of Zen,* McGraw-Hill Paperbacks (New York: McGraw-Hill, 1964), pp. 116-17.

2. From *Living Flame of Love,* Stanza the First. Cf. *The Complete Works of Saint John of the Cross, Doctor of the Church,* trans. and ed. E. Allison Peers. New ed. rev. (London: Burns and Oates, 1953), vol. 3, pp. 21, 22.

3. From "The Sermons." Cf. *Meister Eckhart: A Modern Translation* by Raymond Bernard Blakney, Harper Torchbooks (New York: Harper & Row, 1941), pp. 203,206.

4. Thomas Merton, *Zen and the Birds of Appetite* (New York: New Directions, 1968), pp. 73-4. Merton's italics.

5. For a treatment of freedom, see J.B. Metz, "Freiheit als philosophischtheologisches Grenzproblem" in *Gott in Welt: Festgabe für Karl Rahner* I (Freiburg: Herder, 1964), pp. 287-314.

6. Rudolf Bultmann, "Christianity as a Religion of East and West" in his book, *Essays Philosophical and Theological* (New York: Macmillan, 1955), pp. 220-1. My account of the origins of Christian individualism is drawn from that essay of Bultmann.

7. *Ibid.*, p. 224. Bultmann's italics.

8. *Ibid.*, p. 225.

9. The phrase is Thomas Prufer's in his essay, "A Protreptic: What is Philosophy?" in *Studies in Philosophy and the History of Philosophy*, 2 (Washington: Catholic University Press, 1963), p. 6.

10. *Expositions on the Book of Psalms by S. Augustine of Hippo,* vol. 2, A Library of the Fathers (Oxford, 1848), pp. 193-4. In the English translation the psalm is numbered XLII. (Italics in the original.)

11. The translation quoted is that of F. J. Sheed (London: Sheed & Ward, 1943), p. 137.

12. *A Protreptic,* p. 6.

13. *Expositions on the Book of Psalms by S. Augustine of Hippo,* vol. 3, A Library of the Fathers (Oxford, 1849), p. 64. The quotation is from the commentary on Psalm LV. English numbering, LVI.

14. *St. Augustin: On the Holy Trinity. Doctrinal Treatises. Moral Treatises,* A Select Library of the Nicene and Post-Nicene Fathers of the Christian Church, ed. Philip Schaff, vol. 3 (Buffalo: The Christian Literature Co., 1887), p. 141. The quotation is from Book X, X, 13.

15. That is the contention of Thomas Prufer, *A Protreptic,* pp. 8-9.

16. J. Hillis Miller, "The Poetry of Reality" in his book, *Poets of Reality: Six Twentieth-Century Writers* (Cambridge, Massachusetts: The Belknap Press of Harvard University Press, 1965). p. 2. See also his earlier book, *The Disappearance of God* (Cambridge, Massachusetts: The Belknap Press of Harvard University Press, 1963).

17. *Ibid.,* p. 3.

18. *Ibid.,* pp. 3-4.

19. From "Large Red Man Reading," *The Collected Poems of Wallace Stevens* (London: Faber and Faber, 1945), p. 423.

20. *Poets of Reality,* p. 8.

21. *Ibid.,* p. 9.

22. *Ibid.,* p. 10.

23. *Collected Poems,* pp. 471-2.

24. Frederick Franck, *The Zen of Seeing, seeing/drawing as Meditation,* Vintage Books (New York: Random House, 1973), pp. 5-6.

25. *Ibid.,* p. 11.

Notes to Chapter IV
DEATH AND THE SELF

1. Cf. Rudolf Bultmann, *Essays: Philosophical and Theological* (New York: Macmillan, 1955), p. 224.

2. Cf. E. H. Schillebeeckx, O.P., "The Death of a Christian—I: The Objective Fact," *Life of the Spirit,* 16 (1962), pp. 271-2.

3. The quotation is from the Jerusalem Bible.

4. For a useful brief account, see Ninian Smart, "Attitudes towards death in eastern religions" in Arnold Toynbee and others, *Man's Concern with Death* (London: Hodder and Stoughton, 1968), pp. 95-115.

5. Anchor Books (Garden City, New York: Doubleday, 1967).

6. Cf. Daniel C. Maguire, *Death by Choice* (Garden City, New York: Doubleday, 1974).

7. Elisabeth Kübler-Ross, *On Death and Dying* (London: Tavistock Publications, 1970), p. 13.

8. Alan W. Watts, *Nature, Man and Woman,* Vintage Books (New York: Random House, 1970), pp. 98-9.

9. *Ibid.,* pp. 101-2.

10. Cf. Alan W. Watts, *Beyond Theology: The Art of Godmanship,* Vintage Books (New York: Random House, 1973), p. 125.

11. *Ibid.,* pp. 157-8.

12. *Ibid.,* pp. 47-8.

13. William Hamilton, *On Taking God Out of the Dictionary* (New York: McGraw-Hill, 1974), pp. 75-6.

14. St. Augustine, *The City of God,* Everyman's Library (London: Dent, 1945), vol. 2, p. 58.

15. *St. Augustin: On the Holy Trinity. Doctrinal Treatises. Moral Treatises,*

A Select Library of the Nicene and Post-Nicene Fathers of the Christian Church, ed. Philip Schaff, vol. 3 (Buffalo: The Christian Literature Co., 1887), p. 72. The quotation is from *De Trinitate* Book IV, III, 6.

16. Hans Jonas, *Philosophical Essays: From Ancient Creed to Technological Man* (Englewood Cliffs, New Jersey: Prentice-Hall, Inc., 1974), p. 187. Jonas's italics.

17. *Ibid.,* p. 191. Jonas's italics.

18. *Ibid.,* p. 204.

19. *On Death and Dying,* p. 34.

20. Cf. the remarks of Schillebeeckx to that effect in "The Death of a Christian—II: Our Personal Approach," *Life of the Spirit,* 16 (1962), pp. 337-8.

21. Daniel C. Maguire, *Death by Choice* (Garden City, New York: Doubleday, 1974). For his rejection of biological determinism, see page 142.

22. John S. Dunne, *Time and Myth* (Garden City, New York: Doubleday, 1973), pp. 11-2.

23. Karl Rahner, *On the Theology of Death,* Quaestiones Disputatae, 2 (Edinburgh-London: Nelson, 1961).

24. *Ibid.,* p. 27.

25. Alan W. Watts, *Beyond Theology,* p. 158.

26. *On Death and Dying, passim.*

Notes to Chapter V
THE INHUMANITY OF EVIL

1. Arthur Janov, *The Primal Scream: Primal Therapy, the Cure for Neurosis* (New York: Delta, 1970).

2. *Ibid.,* pp. 9-10.

3. See T. O. Ling, *Buddhism and the Mythology of Evil: A Study in Theravāda Buddhism* (London: Allen & Unwin, 1962). For the comparison between Māra and Satan, see chapter 5.

4. Alan W. Watts, *The Two Hands of God: The Myths of Polarity* (New York: Braziller, 1963). He also touches upon the same theme in his other writings.

5. Cf. Alan Watts, *Beyond Theology: The Art of Godmanship,* Vintage Books (New York: Random House, 1973), p. 33.

6. *The Two Hands of God,* pp. 39-40.

7. See the account of Chrysostom's denunciations and the references in Edward H. Flannery, *The Anguish of the Jews: Twenty-three Centuries of Anti-Semitism,* Quest Books (New York: Macmillan, 1965), pp. 47-9.

8. I quote the phrase from Alan Watts, *The Two Hands of God,* p. 41.

9. Trevor Ling, *The Significance of Satan: New Testament Demonology and its Contemporary Relevance* (London: S.P.C.K., 1961).

10. *Ibid.,* p. 83.

11. Paul Ricoeur, *The Symbolism of Evil,* Beacon Paperback (Boston: Beacon Press, 1969), pp. 257-8. Italics in the original.

12. *Ibid.,* pp. 239-40.

13. *Ibid.,* p. 313.

14. *Ibid.,* p. 314.

15. Alan W. Watts, *Nature, Man and Woman* (New York: Random House, 1970), p. 134.

16. *Ibid.,* p. 346.

17. Frederick Sontag, *The God of Evil: An Argument from the Existence of the Devil* (New York: Harper & Row, 1970), p. 130. Italics in the original.

18. Petru Dumitriu, *Incognito* (London: Collins, 1964), p. 404.

19. *Ibid.,* p. 407.

20. *Ibid.,* p. 458.

21. From "Little Gidding." *Collected Poems 1909-1962* (London: Faber and Faber, 1963), p. 219.

Notes to Chapter VI

SEX: LOVE AND SIN

1. William Empson, *Milton's God,* Rev. ed. (London: Chatto & Windus, 1965), p. 251.

2. *Ibid.,* p. 252.

3. R. P. Lawson in his Introduction in *Origen: The Song of Songs: Commentary and Homilies,* Ancient Christian Writers, 26 (Westminster, Maryland: Newman, 1957), p. 6.

4. *Ibid.,* pp. 22-3.

5. *In Praise of Krishna: Songs from the Bengali.* Trans. Edward C. Dimock, Jr., and Denise Levertov. Anchor Books (Garden City, New York: Doubleday, 1967), p. 56.

6. Stanzas at the beginning of *Ascent of Mount Carmel.* Cf. *The Complete Works of Saint John of the Cross, Doctor of the Church,* trans. and ed. E. Allison Peers New ed. rev. (London: Burns and Oates, 1953), vol. 1, p. 10.

7. Alan Watts lists nine main factors. See *Nature, Man and Woman,* Vintage Books (New York: Random House, 1970), pp. 167-8.

8. *The Four Loves,* Fontana Books (London: Collins, 1963).

9. C. S. Lewis, *Mere Christianity* (New York: Macmillan, 1958), p. 75.

10. *Ibid.*

11. *Out of the Silent Planet* (London: Pan Books, 1952), p. 86.

12. C. S. Lewis, *The Great Divorce* (New York: Macmillan, 1946).

13. *Mere Christianity,* p. 75.

14. For the influence of sexual attitudes upon the relative evaluation and pursuit of different modes of knowledge, Karl Stern, *The Flight from Woman* (New York: Farrar, Straus and Giroux, 1965).

15. Morley Callaghan, *The Loved and the Lost,* Laurentian Library 9 (Toronto: Macmillan, 1970). See chapter 24.

16. Joseph Heller, *Something Happened,* (New York: Knopf, 1974).

17. For the criterion of existential disablement, Roger Balducelli, "Decision for Celibacy," *Theological Studies,* 36 (1975), (Baltimore: Theological Studies, Inc.), pp. 219-42.

18. *In Praise of Krishna.* p. 65.

Notes to Chapter VII
TOWARD A CRITIQUE OF
RELIGIOUS EXPERIENCE

1. For an interpretation of Kant that considers the full scope of his critical philosophy against the restrictive interpretations of the neo-Kantians, see Lucien Goldmann, *Introduction à la philosophie de Kant,* Collection Idées (Editions Gallimard, 1967). For the Kantian revolution as the liberation of reflection against pre-given reality, together with the lack of recognition by Kant himself that critical thought is about history, see Jeremy J. Shapiro, "From Marcuse to Habermas," *Continuum* 9 (1971), 65-6. An English translation of Kant's writings on history, including "What is Enlightenment?" is given in Immanuel Kant, *On History,* edited with an introduction by Lewis White Beck, The Library of Liberal Arts (Indianapolis/New York: Bobbs-Merrill, 1963).

2. Paul Ricoeur, "Philosophy and Religious Language," *The Journal of Religion,* 54 (1974), 73.

3. Susan Sontag, *Against Interpretation and Other Essays,* Second Laurel Edition (New York: Dell, 1969), p. 23. Sontag's italics.

4. For an account of their work, see Martin Jay, *The Dialectical Imagination: A History of the Frankfurt School and the Institute of Social Research 1923-1950* (Boston: Little, Brown & Co., 1973), especially chapter 6: "Aesthetic Theory and the Critique of Mass Culture," pp. 173-218.

5. Cf. *An Essay on Liberation* (Boston: Beacon Press, 1969).

6. J. B. Metz, "Grond en functie van de politieke theologie," *Tijdschrift voer Theologie,* 12 (1972), p. 161.

7. H. Schaeffer, " 'Politieke theologie' in een tijd van 'religieuze renaissance'," *Tijdschrift voor Theologie,* 12 (1972), pp. 239-40.

8. For a good discussion of the issues, see chapter 6: "Religion and Materialism on the Psychoanalyst's Couch" in John Wren-Lewis, *What Shall We Tell the Children?* (London: Constable, 1971), pp. 55-73.

9. William Lynch, *Christ and Prometheus* (Notre Dame, Indiana: University of Notre Dame Press, 1970).

10. *Ibid.,* p. 7.

11. *Ibid.,* p. 27. Lynch's italics.

12. *Ibid.,* p. 31.

13. *Ibid.,* p. 26.

14. *What Shall We Tell the Children?* (London: Constable, 1971), p. 21. Wren-Lewis's italics.

15. For an account of this, together with a discussion of its relevance to theology, see Charles Davis, "Theology and Praxis," *Cross Currents,* 23 (1973), 154-168.

16. *Tell the Children,* p. 62.

17. Lucien Goldmann, *Le Dieu caché: Etude sur la vision tragique dans les Pensées de Pascal et dans le théâtre de Racine* (Editions Gallimard, 1959).

18. A recent example is David B. Burrell, *Exercises in Religious Understanding* (Notre Dame: University of Notre Dame Press, 1974). At the time of writing I have not yet read David Tracy, *Blessed Rage for Order: The New Pluralism in Theology* (New York: The Seabury Press, 1975), but in David Tracy, "Theology as Public Discourse," *The Christian Century,* 19 March, 1975, it is said to be a presentation of five major models for fundamental theology: the orthodox, the liberal, the neo-orthodox, the radical, and the revisionist.

19. Cf. M.D. Chenu, *Introduction à l'étude de Saint Thomas d'Aquin* (Paris: Gabalda, 1950).

20. Cr. M. Xhaufflaire & K. Derksen, *eds., Les Deux visages de la théologie de la sécularisation,* l'actualité religieuse, 29 (Tournai: Casterman, 1970).

21. Jürgen Habermas, "Zur logik der Sozialwissenschaften," *Philosophische Rundschau,* Beiheft 5, Febr. 1967; and *Erkenntnis und Interesse* (Frankfurt-am-Main: Suhrkamp, 1968). For a brief account in English, see Trent Schroyer, "Marx and Habermas," *Continuum* 9 (1971), 52-64.

22. J.B. Metz, "Freiheit als philosophisch-theologisches Grenzproblem" in *Gott in Welt: Festgabe für Karl Rahner* I (Freiburg: Herder, 1964), pp. 287-314.

23. Cf. his essay, "Kirchliche Autorität im Anspruch der Freiheitsgeschichte" in Johann Baptist Metz, Jurgen Moltmann, Willi Oelmüller, *Kirche im Prozesz der Aufklärung: Aspekte einer neuen "politischen Theologie" Gesellschaft und Theologie, Systematische Beiträge,* Nr. 1 (München: Kaiser/Mainz: Grünewald, 1970).

24. Cf. Willi Oelmüller, *Die unbefriedigte Aufklärung: Beiträge zu einer Theorie der Moderne von Lessing, Kant and Hegel* (Frankfurt-am-Main: Suhrkamp, 1969); id., *Was ist heute Aufklärung?* (Düsseldorf: Patmos, 1972).

25. Robert Morgan, "Expansion and Criticism in the Christian Tradition" in *The Cardinal Meaning; Essays in Comparative Hermeneutics: Buddhism and Christianity,* Michael Pye and Robert Morgan, *eds.,* (The Hague/Paris: Mouton, 1973), p. 84.

26. *Ibid.,* p. 101.

Index